VASILIS

A true story of faith, adventure and commitment
(The blazing trail of a journey of faith)

To Sister ANNA WEBB-MORRIS

God Bless

Konstantopoulos 10-6-19

Thank you for great
Music

By Dr. Bill C. Konstantopoulos

Vasilis: A true story of faith, adventure and commitment
ISBN: 978-1-60416-527-2

First Printing April 2011

Reformation Publishers
242 University Drive,
Prestonsburg, Kentucky 41653
1-800-765-2464

rpublisher@aol.com
www.reformationpublishers.com

Book design by Michael Belcher
Edited by Donald Neace

Printed in the United States of America
POD: LSI

GREECE – Vasilis' Homeland

Mar's Hill

"And when he had gone over those parts, and had given them much exhortation, he came into Greece..." Acts 20:2. "The same came therefore to Philip, which was of Bethsaida of Galilee, and desired him, saying, Sir, we would see Jesus"

John 12:21.

Vasilis on Acropolis, looking at Parthenon, which overshadows Mar's Hill

"And the time of ignorance God winked at: but now commandeth all men everywhere to repent: Because he hath appointed a day, in the which he will judge the world in righteousness by that man whom he hath ordained; whereof he hath given assurance unto all men, in that he hath raised him from the dead" Acts 17:30-31.

**In loving memory of my parents who loved me
unconditionally
Dinos A. Konstantopoulos and Dina Konstantopoulos**

"Blessed are the poor in spirit, for theirs in the kingdom of heaven."

In humble gratitude to my two brothers and sister
who have supported me sacrificially:
Thanasis Konstantopoulos, Christos Konstantopoulos,
and Yeota Asteri Konstantopoulos

Christos   Yeota   Thanasis   Vasilis

"Behold how good it is for brethren to dwell together in unity."

6

In loving memory of my sister-in-law, Thanasis' wife, who supported Vasilis' dream and who served all sacrificially, but never had the opportunity to see Vasilis' dream be fulfilled or her five small children to grow up. She died at the age of 32. Eleni Mbaka Konstantopoulos.

Tuola, Elias, Daniel, Thanasis, Stefanos and Dina

Table of Contents

Forward

To see God, the creator of the world interacting in the life of a human being, is both a miraculous and a marvelous story. The Scriptures are full of examples of how individuals developed powerful and impactful relationships with our Lord. Abraham, Moses, David, and Paul are just a few examples of the transformative work that can occur when the servant truly seeks, in obedience and love, a deeply-committed relationship with God.

The life story of Bill C. Konstantopoulos (Bill K.) is an example today of the power and fulfillment found in a Christ-centered life. Gripped by the awesome idea and total commitment to the grand plan of the Master Designer, Bill K. is an example today of the seed which fell on good soil and multiplied greatly (Matt 13–8). You will be inspired by reading how, through prayer and total reliance on Christ, Bill K. was able to overcome the adversities of life in a fallen world. His story is inspirational for both the new and mature Christian.

I recommend the reading of Bill K's story because it will be transforming as you see how God has led this faithful servant in the past, and how he continues to lead him today. It is a testimony to the steadfastness of God being faithful to those who trust entirely in his word, and ever-abiding presence.

It has been my joy to work personally with Bill K. and walk alongside him for over a decade in the national ministry of the Church of God. I have been blessed by his servant leadership, commitment to Christ, and love for his fellow man. And now having read his life story, I am doubly blessed by his living testimony. I am sure you will be, too.

Ronald V. Duncan, D. Min
General Director
Church of God Ministries

PROLOGUE

It was a little more than 48 years ago when Vasilis first set foot on the soil of the United States of America. From the early days where God allowed him to share the work of His grace in his life and the process through which His providence had led, people from all directions urged him to put the story into print. The desire was to unfold the manner in which Vasilis' life has been shaped by God's love, directed by the Holy Spirit and seasoned by the principles of His word. All those years he resisted with the excuse, "Some day probably I will."

Time has moved swiftly and it has been more than 48 years since he first uttered those words. The journey now appears to be getting closer to its destination. Even though the spirit of faith, adventure and commitment have not diminished, it seems that the rays of hope rise stronger than ever as the anchor of the soul envisions that which is coming as a result of that which has taken place by the grace of God.

At the urging of his wife and others, it appeared that it was time to revisit the journey which has been long, wide, and treacherous sometimes and triumphant most of the time. It is time to be reexamined and recorded for memory's sake and with the hope and prayer that it will be a challenge and an inspiration to fellow pilgrims in life. Thanks to Kay, in the spring of 2009 they marked 35 days on the calendar to make a solo trip to Greece and the place of Vasilis' birth. The trip was back to the village where both his childhood and youth were shaped and where the grace of God visited and where his journey in the kingdom and for the kingdom began.

As he reflects on those early moments and on the humble beginning of his existence, his heart still leaps with joy and gratitude with the words ringing like bells in his ears, "Who am I, that I have been given the privilege to roam the world with the King and for the King?" "Who am I, to have the opportunity to embrace countries and cultures, languages and lands, brotherhood and barriers, with the excitement of a child and the wonder that continues to thrill my soul?" "Amazing grace, how sweet the sound that saved a wretch like me, I once was lost but now I am found, was blind but now I see."[1]

Considering the place where he was born, the circumstances that surrounded his existence, the family conditions and the events which time after time endeavored to annihilate his family, still he raises the question, "Who am I, to be endued with divine grace and be honored in such a significant way with a message and a ministry?"

On May 25, 2009, Vasilis reluctantly kissed his wife goodbye and boarded the airplane with the excitement of a child for a land and a people who have always been in his memory, but whose images began to fade. It reminded him of 48 years earlier. That flight had been full of faith, anxiousness and expectation, following what he had perceived to be God's call for his life to an unknown land and circumstances. Looking back it was a most adventurous thing to fly across the ocean for the first time to a place where he knew no one. He had flown confidant of the companionship of The One whose hand led him. What a great surprise and adventure was waiting!

The first eight days were spent with his older brother, Christos and his wife Foteni, in Linkoping, Sweden, where they tried to reconnect and refresh memories about the old days in the place of childhood. Memories corrected each other on faulty information as they relived childhood experiences. Together they laughed, cried, sighed and breathed thanks and gratitude for the hand of providence, with the agreement that it was unconditional love in the family and the hand of divine grace that resulted in the survival of the family.

On June 4th, Vasilis arrived in Greece, the land of his birth, and spent time with his brother Thanasis and his sister

Yeota. He was armed with a host of questions and the intense desire to remember. They spent many hours past midnight expressing all kinds of emotions. Questions and answers flowed like drops of rain, reviving childhood memories of hardship long submerged in their coconscious minds. They revisited the place of their birth, Agridion. There, they roamed its hills, often without shoeless, grasping for the fruit of a cherry or pear, as they triedg to understand the horrors of the German War (WWII), the devastation and depression that pushed the family in all four directions, followed by civil war that seemed certain to annihilate the whole family.

They talked with young and old, met old friends and relatives long forgotten; they listened to story after story which brought tears, laughter and often deep sighs. They visited the graves of Mom and Dad and sister-in-law, which brought them to a moment of silence, sobriety and reflection. Life never stands still. Some nurture their wounds; others count their victories. Some reflect on the past while others envision the future. Some are overtaken by the loss and pain, but others dream of brighter moments and hope for a better tomorrow. As for them, they were overwhelmed with silence, reverence, respect and reflection, as the words resounded in their minds, "Thro' many dangers, toils and snares, I have already come: 'Tis grace hath bro't me safe thus far, and grace will lead me home." [2]

The most rewarding moments were those passed around the table. They ate delicious meals, laughed, cried, and shared stories about each other long forgotten. They read from the Word, they sang and prayed; and reflected on the grace of God that visited the family in the most difficult and dangerous times. They reflected on how His grace has been the sustaining force through the years. It was grace that mapped the journey, marked the stations and ordered their steps. They could say with certainty, "Hitherto the Lord has been with us." "We have come this far by faith, leaning on the Lord." So, brace yourself as we go through the following pages, which will give you a feel of the times, the places, the circumstances and the family of Vasilis. But beyond that, you will find yourself merging into the details of Vasilis' life and the journey of faith; and you will be convinced that it is a life, as Verna Joiner wrote several years ago in the "Sunday School Times" magazine, "Led by His Hand." [3]

As the events and the expressions of Vasilis' life are penned down in a way that memory facilitates them, whether they will be sad, glad or humorous or if there would be an occasional "praise the Lord" or "thank the Lord"; there is a twofold motive in putting the story together, a motive for which Vasilis has given his life. First, is for Jesus Christ, our Lord and King, to be glorified and exalted. It is He who has redeemed Vasilis and has been the captain of his voyage. He has been the guide and the source of strength, whose faithfulness has been reliable at all times. Second, it is his hope that fellow pilgrims, just like Vasilis, who struggle with life's questions and are confronted with burdens which are hard to bear, that they will be encouraged and strengthened to make Jesus Christ the pilot of their life and fully trust in the everlasting arms of the Great I AM whose arm is never shortened that cannot save.

The thrust of this story is that no matter what your circumstances, the place of your birth, your family background, your failures, the conditions of the times in which you live and the mountain-like obstacles that you face, you can overcome, you can soar with the eagles and you can be used to bless to the measure of your faith in Christ and the surrender and abandonment of yourself to Him. With Christ every tragedy and every calamity in life bears the inscription, "There is hope, Hope in God" (Ps. 42:5 NKJV).

What you will read in the following pages is a true story; with the exception if memory is faulty with some small details, which could be rare but possible. Some of the events described could be viewed differently by others, but such differences neither changes them nor alters their reality. It is not the intent to present a perfect story without flaws or failures, the focus of the story is on the adventure of faith that enables us to be more than conquerors and a grace that is sufficient for all our shortcoming and even failures.

Come as we travel together the path of memory and as we stop from time to time in some of the stations of life which could cause a tear, a smile and possibly a sigh, but the overall feel will be, "His grace is sufficient, Praise the Lord, the journey has been worth all effort, pain, loss and sacrifice and its gains outweigh everything else." Come -- Ελα μαζιμου -- ela mazimou, let's relive the journey together!

ACKNOWLEDGEMENTS

The late senator from Carolina, Jessie Helms said once, *If you see a turtle sitting on a tree stump, you know that it did not get there all by itself.* This means there is not anyone in life who achieves anything of great significance without the assistance of someone else. There is an undeniable interdependence in life that ought to keep all of us humble. None of us is fully self-sufficient. It is the kindness and the contribution of others in our life that help us to climb some mountains, cross some rivers and overcome some obstacles in life. It could be in the form of an encouraging word, a gesture of giving or an act of kindness; but all had the same effect, encouraging us to go forward, inspiring us to press toward the mark.

Even though this is the recount of a story, there are many who have contributed to its making and credit must be given to where credit is due. Vasilis' heart is grateful to his parents who loved him unconditionally and who contributed honesty, integrity, love for people and positive outlook in life, in spite of its events and circumstances. Their example even before they were Christians impacted his life in the most positive way.

His heartfelt thanks to his brothers Thanasis and Christos and his sister Yeota who not only supported him sacrificially in all his endeavors, but also contributed so much to refresh his memory and in filling in the gap with some details of the story which had escaped this world- traveling boy. Their honest input and hospitable spirit not only restored some information but also refreshed the soul.

A sense of deep gratitude and thanks is owed to Kay, the wonderful wife who provided encouragement through the years to put the story into print. She made sure he found the time, even going through the painful effort locating the photo boxes and selecting the pictures that make this story come alive. Her reading of the first draft of the manuscript, her recommendations and suggestions greatly helped.

A great deal is owed to providential angels who assisted so much in God's plan for Vasilis' life and who contributed not only to his well being, but also to the shape and direction of the development of the ministry that God has given him. They are too numerous to mention and they come from all walks of life, different countries and from all over America. Some played a more significant role, others an auxiliary one, but all were used by God to set the perimeters so that Vasilis could march to the drumbeat of God's purpose. The memory of some is so vivid for Vasilis that there is not any doubt that God has ordained them. They were in the place and the time which God had appointed and they were faithful in executing that which God had promised.

A word of thanks is due to my former church secretary, Ruth Ann Sartain, who has labored tirelessly in typing the manuscript.

Last but not least I am indebted to Pastor Don Neace, former state minister and editor of *Reformation Witness*, for doing the primary editing of the manuscript.

1. John Newton, Amazing Grace! *Worship the Lord, Hymnal of the Church of God*, Warner Press, Anderson, Indiana, 1989, No. 127.
2. John Newton
3. Verna Joiner, *Greek Teen-Ager Led by A Voice,* The Sunday School Times and Gospel Herald, July 1, 1971, pp 10-11,15, Union Press.

THE STORY

"Another story, Mama?" That was the common expression heard around the fireplace night after night as the wind was beating against our modest home. The house was built from stone with a ceramic roof; a two story facility. The lower part was for the animals and the upper for the family. The fireplace was the only heat for the house and it was the most common place for the family to get together to engage in conversation, play games and exchange information which had arrived in the small village from persons who had traveled outside the village.

The fireplace was the platform for many informative and sometimes motivational stories filled with faith, inspiration and adventure. Vasilis' mother was a powerful storyteller. Even though she lacked formal education and the experience of a traveling person, her stories were powerful and moving. As the blanket of darkness continued to cover this mountainous village, and the bleating of the sheep had ceased, the fireplace had become the most vibrant place for the family. In the midst of popping firewood and flying sparks would come a loud and clear challenge, "Another story, Mama?"

So the stories continued with the most powerful teaching tool till the fire died out and the clock would have stricken midnight, but there was no clock to do so.
It was in this kind of setting that Vasilis' mind was cultivated and his heart was warmed and inspired by stories. As a result of it, he became a lover of stories. Later as he grew up and became mature in the faith, he sought refuge in the stories of men who fought the odds of life, overcame obstacles, conquered impossibilities, found peace and life's direction as well as having an encounter with the divine. The stories of saints, reformers, adventurous persons, and specially the stories of persons with handicaps to whom the world gave little chance, always inspired his soul and challenged his mind to

press forward without accepting the limitations placed on him by people or circumstances.

Stories are the best means of communication. They show us the struggles, the efforts, the defeats and the triumphs of people under diverse circumstances, and how they handled the tearing and hurting things of life. Stories serve as a mirror where we can see ourselves and both challenge and inspire us. Everyone has a story. If we know the story of a person, that knowledge will shape our attitude toward that person. For some it is a story of constant struggle, defeat, anguish and pain. For others it is a story of joy, triumph and constant advance, but everyone has a story. Whether the story is decorated with defeats or triumphs, with pain or joy, with fame or obscurity, does not make much difference. The difference in a story is made whether it is related or not to the Big Story; the story of God's love as revealed in the person of Jesus Christ. You see when our story is touched by the Big Story; it is not only changed but also receives meaning and significance. In these pages we will be sharing Vasilis' story of faith, adventure and commitment; but only as related to the Big Story. Because Vasilis' story, had it not been affected by the Big Story, we would not have much of a story to share, had it not been for the Big Story; only we would recount events which could or could not have any great significance.

As these lines are written the mind runs through the pages of the Bible and even church history, searching for stories which have been affected by the Big Story. Who could tell us what the story of Abraham would have been like if it had not been touched by the Big Story of love and faithfulness and if he had not said yes to the Big Story? What would we be sharing today about Moses, that stuttering shepherd, if he had not had an encounter with the Big Story of God's redemptive purpose in the event of the burning bush? Would he have been forgotten and lost in the bleating of the sheep without neither Egypt or Israel have ever seen his face or heard his voice?

Would there ever have been an Exodus, a dividing of the sea, manna from heaven or water from the rock? What story would we be sharing today about Moses if he had not been touched by the Big Story? What story would we be telling today about Saul of Tarsus, the persecutor of the church and the denier of Christ, if he had not been touched on the Damascus Road by the Big Story of God's redemptive love as it is revealed in the death and the resurrection of Jesus Christ? Would there have been a Mar's Hill discourse, a Philippi miracle, and the Ephesus uproar, a reference to the Unknown God and a call to repentance? Would he have been lost in the pages of pagan history as the one who persecuted the Way and who had consented at Stephen's death? What would have been the story of Martin Luther, the monk who was dissatisfied and discontented both with his life and the church, if there had not been an encounter with the Big Story, "the just shall live by faith"?

We do not know what the stories of these men would have been, but we do know what they are, simply because they have been touched by the Big Story of God's redeeming love and life, conduct and destiny have been shaped by it. So, in these pages we will be telling Vasilis' story that has become possible because of the Big Story. Whether we would talk about struggles and strengths, tests and tears, faith and fears, success and failures, obstacles and opportunities, all will be related to the Big Story, the story of God's amazing love and grace. In the meantime the word of John Newton would be hovering over us like a security blanket, "Twas grace that taught my heart to fear, and grace my fears relieved; how precious did that grace appear, the hour I first believed!" [1]

1. John Newton.

THE PLACE

The place where Vasilis was born is a small picturesque village in the mountains of Southern Greece. The south part of Greece called Peloponnesus is rich in history and it is divided from the mainland by the Corinthian Isthmus, a manmade canal in the 1800s and it resembles an oak leaf. It is surrounded by ocean. It was in this area where the Spartan Kingdom was located and where the Ancient Olympic Games began. It was in this area that the Byzantine Emperor moved his headquarters after his defeat with the hope that he could regroup and regain power. It was in this part of the country that the revolt against the Ottoman Empire (Turks) took place and where a lot of historical events were born. In fact this area has been fertilized with the blood of Greek heroes whose monuments decorate the area.

Vasilis' village

The village in which Vasilis lived is located in the mountainous area in the state of Arcadia and the county of Gordinia. Its name is Agridion, which means a small place or garden. Its history is long and rich. Its beginning goes back at

22

least 1000 or 1200 years. Its beginning is rather uncertain. Some say that it was established by the Byzantine Emperor by building a monastery there and sent a wealthy fellow there with the name Nifonas who established a community in the form of a beautiful garden, but nothing is certain. In its prime the village has had 150 to 200 families, but at the time of Vasilis 50 to 70. It is said that at one time there were 10,000 to 15,000 sheep and goats grazing on the hillside. Another story says that a shepherd was grazing his flock in that area who noticed that his leading goat had disappeared one day and upon returning he saw its beard to be wet. The following day he followed the goat which led him to a gushing water fountain on the side of the mountain. It was around that fountain that the village was established. The water fountain still exists today in the center of the village. Even though the time and the manner of the establishment of the village are uncertain, its vitality and historical significance are not.[1]

The vrisi – fountain Christos, Thanasis, Yeota & Sakis

The village had become a close community which gave the impression of a large family of hard-working, honest, God-

23

fearing people bound together by a common cause and whose hospitality, kindness and cooperation were extended to all. At the time of Vasilis' birth, the village was practically untouched by civilization. There was no radio or TV, no phones and no road or cars. The only roads were small paths that people would travel by foot, donkey, mule or horse to the city of Tripoli and the valley called cambos. It was not uncommon for people to walk three and four hours in order to go to other towns for mere necessities. In those days, Thursday was the most exciting day of the week, the mail man would come on horseback and after he had parked his horse on the main village square that was in the front of the church, he would blow his horn and the villagers would come to get their mail and send mail.

The old school

There was no running water, electricity, toiletry or any other conveniences of life. The most common place where the people would gather was the vrisi, water fountain. It was there that families received water, watered their flocks and where the exchange

The Renovated School

of information took place. There was a one room school, a

24

church called Agia Triada, Holy Trinity, at which every year would have a celebration for two or three days, called panigiri with abundance of food and entertainment for all who came without a charge.

There were a couple of alonia, places where people thrashed their wheat, barley and oats. Even though the main livestock were sheep and goats, history records at one time there were a thousand cattle roaming the hillside. The village is overshadowed by a high mountain called vlogos in the language of the people from which derive a host of legends. There was a cafenio, café and a small grocery store with the bare necessities where at times you bought things by trading other products like eggs.

This small village both experienced and endured the tragedy of war and all sorts of calamities. It survived the Turkish occupation and there were twenty men from the village who had joined Colocotronis's revolt against the Turks in 1821, some of whom had high ranks in the revolutionary army. During World War II, it was invaded by the Germans and as it was their style they set on fire the main buildings of the village and executed the men whom they could capture. Most of the folks survived by running to the mountains, mostly traveling by night and having watchmen on certain points who observed the movements of the Germans and advised the people accordingly.

The most devastating thing for the village was the civil war from 1944-1949 where neighbors turned against neighbors and family against family. It was during that time that the village suffered the worst, which left deep wounds and scars. Vasilis' family has its share of troubles and suffering during this time. His father was beaten without mercy and was thrown in jail for 18 months. His brother next to the oldest was literally tortured and imprisoned for several months. Also his older brother was detained and threatened. All these together with the depression during that time brought a drastic change in

25

the village and the great exodus began to take place. Some sought refuge in the big cities, others moved to the fertile fields of Southern Greece and a great number of youngsters set their sail for Germany, Australia and even the United States. But the village never lost its appeal and the mood of celebration. The families became fewer and fewer, the laughter of the children quickly died out and soon old and wrinkled faces became the permanent fixtures. The sound of the shepherd's tsouria (flute) ceased to echo throughout the mountains and the miriology (song of mourning) seldom was heard. Occasionally one might hear a clarinet or bouzouki which would set the mood of celebration again.

The Church

But coming panigiri time the celebration could begin and for two days locals and strangers, expatriates and nostalgic travelers, would lose themselves in its warm spirit of hospitality with the feeling of a family which has become small, has been wounded and suffered untold pain, but it managed to survive without losing its spirit. It creates nostalgia for those who have not walked its stony streets for years, to gather in the village on Easter Sunday and sing "Christos anesti" – Christ is risen -- and drink water from the vrisi of the village.

Vasilis' birthplace – house

Time has brought many changes in this small village, but the spirit of generous love and warm hospitality still remain. When you do visit, old and wrinkled faces would embrace you, kiss you on both cheeks, and hold you with both hands on each side of your shoulders and looking you straight in the eyes would engage you in a soul searching conversation. No matter what the time of the day, you would never be allowed to leave without accepting the invitation for dinner or serving you with gluko (dessert). What a place! What a spirit! What a people! Its quietness and scenery could help one recover his soul!

1. Konstantopoulos, Dimitrios, To Agridion Gordinias, Pyrgos 1998, pp. 56-61, 83-94.

THE TIMES

Solomon, from the Bible, the wise man and king of Israel who explored everything and who drunk both from the sweet and bitter cup of life said, "There is a time for everything, a time to laugh and a time to cry, a time to build up and time to tear down that which has been built, time for war and for peace" (Ecclesiastes 3: 1-8).

In 1938 the small village of Agridion with all its serenity, beauty and contentment, was totally unaware of the players who were about to step on the world stage and change the world forever. The coming events also altered the life in the village as it had been known. Mussolini of Italy on the one hand was sharpening his sword and counting his troops as he was envisioning beautiful Greece. Hitler on the other hand had put his chess players in array methodically and strategically on how he was going to conquer the world. Even though after he got out of prison and had published, "My Battle", in which he had outlined his plan and had stated his philosophy, no one had taken him seriously.

Greece at that time was struggling with its own political and economic turmoil. It had barely put behind World War I and was looking forward for some peace and stability; but it was agonizing with an internal political struggle which ended up in a dictatorship in 1938, with Metaxas as the dictator. Since the means of communication were not up to par at that time, it took long time for information to reach the people, it all arrived by word of mouth.

Even though some details about the times will merge in the following pages as we share the story, during Vasilis' most formative years, 1938-1949, were Greece darkest, most painful, devastating, costly and grievous days which altered the political, social, and cultural landscape of the country. There remained no one who was not affected by the dark events of those years. No one knew there were so much hatred,

28

vengeance and ruthlessness that were waiting to be awakened among the Greek people. If the reader is interested in the happenings of that period, it will be helpful if he could read the book Eleni by Nicholas Gage. Even though the book describes life during those years in Albania and Northern Greece, it gives an accurate picture of the mood, the motives and the madness of the people during that time. It describes the madness of the civil war where the enemy is unidentifiable because it resides in friends and family.

When Mussolini mobilized his army and invaded the then Bulgaria, he asked for Greece to surrender, so that he could enter the country freely. Metaxas, Greece dictator, replied with an emphatic, "Ochi" – No. The Greeks were able to repel the Italians who entered Greece from the Albanian border. But when Hitler began to march toward Greece and Metaxas gave him the same emphatic "Ochi" – No – which he had given to Mussolini, the German wrath was unleashed against Greece and within two weeks it fell to the Germans. The government failed, the currency was worthless and the economy in shambles which caused the country to plunge into a painful, prolonged depression that tried the very soul of the people. Several older folks who had shared the horrors of hardship would say, "If it was not for the Marshal Plan of the United States, Greece would have not survived." From the time that Greece was occupied there was resistance in Greece from two fronts. On one side was the Tagmatofilakes or the right, remnants of the army. On the other front was the Antartes or the left. When eventually the Germans withdrew or were defeated, Greece plunged into its darkest hour, a five-year civil war that left the country divided, polarized and as a bouncing ball between the two political powers that used the situation for personal vendettas.

It was this climate, these circumstances and this kind of events that nurtured Vasilis' life and shaped his worldview. It was the devastation of the war and the dehumanization of the depression that caused the great exodus from Greece during that time and afterwards. But the wonderful fact always remains true that divine providence and God's grace always uses such times to form certain individuals and shape their destiny both in the kingdom and for the kingdom. That was the case with Vasilis as our journey will reveal later.

THE FAMILY

Vasilis' family lived in the last house on the southwest side of the village. It was a two story stone house with ceramic roof, two stone porches, one of the east side and the other on the west, and a fourno (clay oven) outside. The water that run from the main vrisi (fountain) formed a small creek in the middle of the family property. The two roads that passed on either side of the house led to the water fountain, the school and the church.

The lower part of the house was used for the animals; a donkey, a mule or a horse, a few goats and sheep and a few chickens. The back part of the house was surrounded with a mantra (stone fence) with a large gate in the center. On the front of the house there was a stone porch with a grapevine on the side, arranged in such a way that it could provide shade for the porch during the summer.

The upper part of the house was divided in two with a wooden wall in the middle. The one side consisted of a fireplace, the kitchen, a wooden table for the family meals and a bed used by Vasilis' Mom and Dad. This was the place where the family spent most of the time together. The winter evenings were spent around the fireplace and the summer nights at the porch visiting with the neighbors. The other side of the house had the beds for the children. There was no electricity, toiletry or running water in the house.

According to the village standards at the time the family was a poor family. They were identified as agrotes (farmers or agriculture people) and as ktinotrofoi (people who tended livestock, primarily sheep and goats). Many of the villagers would travel to the valley of Peloponnesus, called cambos, two or three times a year to supplement their income as laborers in cultivating the vineyards in the spring, harvesting resins and grapes in the late summer and gathering olives in the late fall. All these labors required the participation of the whole family.

Vasilis' family consisted of six (6) people besides himself, His paternal grandmother, the only grandparent that he knew, was a petite, energetic, small lady who did some of the house work while the others were working in the fields. The grandmother, yiayia, as it is called in Greek, also took care of the younger children during the day, and especially Vasilis, the first four years of his life.

Vasilis' father was a tall, thin, light complexioned gentleman with blue eyes, a small mustache, and a touch of gray on his hair. He was full of pride, energy and a personality that brought cheers in whatever location or situation that he found himself. He always had a positive attitude and once confessed he did not know what it meant to worry. He was hardworking, valued character and integrity and

Dinos

his word was a bond. He served in World War I, survived the German war, a depression and a civil war in which he was beaten and imprisoned unjustly. He saw his family suffer great loss and went through several relocations but he never complained. He was always upbeat about life. Even though he was not a Christian by experience, each evening as he lay in bed to sleep he would recite the Lord's Prayer. He had wit, humor and loved the entertainment and social life of the village around ouzo, tsipouro, koniak and the fruit of the vine. Of all the decisions that he made in his lifetime, the best two were the kind of a woman that he married and then at the age of 80 when he gave his heart to the Lord Jesus Christ, accepting Him as his savior and Lord. His life was totally transformed and he lived fifteen years as a transformed man by the grace of God. He went to be with the Lord at the age of 95.

Vasilis' mother was petite, dark complexion with brown eyes surrounded by dark circles and black hair. For all practical purposes she was illiterate, but her wisdom and common sense had no equal. Her unconditional love and spirit of service served as the glue that kept the family together. She was a slave of love and self-sacrifice. Her honesty, integrity and her

Dina

positive attitude with the spirit of self-giving had gained her the reputation that you could trust her with anything. The rumor was that the lights never went out in her house. She would never go to bed until everyone was safe at home. The pain, the loss and the hardship in her life cannot be put into words; but they never affected her spirit and they did not sour her love. She was a God-fearing woman even before she knew the Lord and she pushed education at any cost. She always found ways to illustrate the importance of education and she would make any sacrifice to secure materials which could assist her children.

She gave birth to Vasilis when she was 44 years old and she accepted Christ in her early sixties and became a very intense disciple of Christ and a prayer warrior. Her intense desire for the Word of God led her to learn to read in her seventies and before her death had read through a large print abbreviated Bible with pictures. She went to be with the Lord when she was 84 and it was her devotion and her life that led her husband to the Lord after her death. Her words to him every night that they went to bed were these, "Dino, repent before it is too late!"

Thanasis

Vasilis' oldest brother is named Thanasis. Thanasis is about 5.6 feet, dark complexion and brown eyes with dark hair. He is very methodical, well organized, thoughtful and progressive with a keen mind and the gift of practical wisdom. He had religious tendencies early in his life and his beautiful voice opened the door for him in an early age to be a psaltis (singer) in the Greek Orthodox Church. It was not songs that they were singing in the Greek Orthodox Church but the Gospels in an antiphonic way. Thanasis assumed the leadership and the initiative for the family during the civil war while the father was in prison. He could be credited for the survival of the family. The survival of the family is owed to his love, self-sacrifice and wisdom. The German war left him with one eye due to a land mine accident and his many hardships and difficulties would sound like tales to most people. But his optimism combined with character, integrity, honesty and endless hard work help him rise above every calamity and earned him the respect and trust of all.

His acceptance of Christ in the early 1950s totally transformed his life. He not only became a faithful man, but also a fervent evangelist both with the spoken word, the distribution of the printed word and as the pastor of a small congregation. He has turned 82 years old, but his fervent zeal for evangelism and Christian hospitality still are the passions of his soul. He is married to Soteroula and he has five children with his first wife, Eleni, who died at the age of 32. His children's names are Toula, Stefanos, Dina, Elias and Daniel.

Christos

Christos is Vasilis' older brother. He is of light complexion, dark eyes and he used to have black hair. He has a plus personality that makes him the life of the party no matter where it is. He never knows a stranger. It is fun to be with him. He is hardworking, positive and generous and trusting to a fault. His loyalty to the family and his sacrificial love has gone beyond the call of duty at difficult times. His childhood was practically nonexistent, filled with hardship, pain and circumstances which were filled with fear and uncertainty. At the age of 13, during the civil war, he was imprisoned and tortured without cause for three months which could have embittered him; but he learned the spirit of forgiveness and how to fight evil with good. He always loves the fun part of life and he engages life to its fullest. His work ethics and his friendship loyalties have earned him a name of respect. His adventurous spirit has taken him to many adventures and in the 1960s he immigrated to Sweden. He is about 79 years old and enjoys retirement with half of the year spent in Greece and the other half in Sweden. He is married to Fotini and they have two daughters, Dina and Olga.

Yeota is Vasilis' older and only sister. She is a carbon copy of her mother both in character, appearance, and demeanor and in the spirit of love and service. She is of dark complexion with brown eyes and long dark hair with a permanent smile and sweet disposition. Vasilis and Yeota grew

Yeota

up together because they are two and a half years apart. Since they are the youngest, they went to school together and they did not have all the work responsibilities like the older children. When she was young she studied to become a seamstress but she never practiced the profession, she just endeavored to meet the needs of the family since everything was made at home.

Later when Yeota gave her heart to the Lord all her God-given qualities were enriched by the Spirit of God. Her devotion to God and His word, her prayer life, her service and hospitality earned her both respect and influence. She is married to Sakis and they have two children, Mimis and Niki and three grandchildren.

Vasilis' family has gone through two wars, plus a depression and several relocations. They suffered loss, separation and pain. More than twice they started all over again with practically nothing. Some were tortured, others were imprisoned and some were separated for prolonged time, but at the end the family emerged stronger, united and bound by an unshakable faith and unbending love. They have been determined not to allow the happening of life to sour their spirit and steal their joy. Things really changed when the members of the family began to accept the Lord. The gates of heaven opened and the Lord showered them with His blessings.

CHILDHOOD AND LIFE IN THE VILLAGE

Vasilis with a revolutionary uniform used in 1821

"Suffer the little children to come unto me, and forbid them not: for of such is the kingdom of God. Verily I say unto you, Whosoever shall not receive the kingdom of God as a little child, he shall not enter therein"

Mark 10:14.

The psalmist says the Lord knew him while he was formed in his mother's womb! Does providence ordain our steps?   The happenings of life – are they accidents or schoolmasters that shape our life by providing lessons for our destiny? If God knows our name, directs our steps and has a unique purpose and plan for our life, then nothing that happens in life is an accident. Everything is directed by divine providence for our making, including dramatic experiences. Even though God does not send bad things, He always uses them to make us and direct us in the path of His plan and purpose. But it is our choices that seal His intentions and make the soul to soar within His will.

It was a cold January night in 1938 where the shepherds had gathered their flocks in their proper abode; the villagers had made their last trip to the vrisi for water before a blanket of darkness covered the remote village of Agridion. Soon light from kerosene lamps began to decorate the village houses. A few men had gathered in the cafenio (café) for a cup of coffee, a game of poker and to catch up with the news of the day. When the cafenio closed the men would walk together on their way home. The silence of the night would be interrupted from time to time with an occasional kalinichta – good night – as each man would break from the group toward his house. There is no doubt that one of those men was Vasilis' father. Soon the lights were out one after the other and the village began to sink into total darkness and silence, with the exception of Vasilis' house.

The father was the last of the men to reach his home since it was located at the end of the southwest part of the village. Not too long after the father had entered the house, his 44 year old wife gave birth to Vasilis.   It was just before midnight on January 30, 1938. It was for that reason that the light had not gone out in that house. Those present to welcome Vasilis into the world were his grandmother Panayeota, his father Dinos, his brothers Thanasis and Christos, and his sister

Yeota. The next day the family received the congratulations of the villagers and there is no doubt that his dad bought drinks for the men in the cafenio and probably passed out cigarettes as it was the custom.

There are very few details of Vasilis' first three years of life. There are no photos or any other memorabilia to reflect or being reminded of those three years. Because the family was of the Greek Orthodox Church, a few weeks after birth they took him to the Church where he was baptized. Infant baptism and the anointing with oil are supposed to make the child a Christian. It was during the baptism that the name of the child was announced. Whosoever from the children could arrive first at Vasilis' house and announce his name would receive a gift which could come in different forms, money or something else. There always was a Godfather and a Godmother, who got involved in the life of the child and quite often during his life, especially in the early years, would shower him or her with gifts. There were times that they would promise to meet some of the needs of the child and in several occasions commitment was made to assist with his education.

Vasilis, being the youngest child of the family, received special attention by all and quite often there were complaints that he was spoiled. There were times when the summer arrived that the mother would take Vasilis with her in the field during the harvest time on a special cot called counia which she hanged from a tree so that the child could be under shade and protected from any crawling creatures. Most of the time he stayed at home and received loving tender care of his grandmother, Panayeota. Since the family was occupied with farming and livestock, they had responsibility seven days a week. There were times that they will leave the house before sunrise and return after sunset.

After work in the field had ended, the normal routine for Vasilis' mother would be to stop to cut firewood and then load herself with it for the 45 minutes or an hour walk home.

She did all her housework in the evening. Once or twice a week she got up at 4:00 a.m. to make bread and bake it outside in a clay oven which had to be fired with wood for almost two hours and most of the time the bread was ready by the time the children got up. One of the fun memories that Vasilis has from while he was growing up, was when he got up in the morning, smell the freshly baked bread and watch his dad churning the milk and making butter. It was his childhood delight to take a piece of freshly baked bread, put fresh butter on it and spray it with sugar. Vasilis' mother made practically everything that the family wore. She wove both cotton and wool from which she made all the clothing and the bedding. Even to this day Vasilis has a couple blankets woven by his mother.

The religious life of the family was that of nominal members of the Greek Orthodox Church (which was the result of being baptized in it). They would attend services on the main holidays such as Christmas, Easter and some saints' holidays, including funerals, baptisms and other special occasions. There were occasions that they would attend church services out in the country when there was a celebration of a certain saint in whose honor a church was built. Normally people who would like to take communion on Easter or Christmas would have to go to the priest for eksomologima (confession). The women would attend church more often than the men. On especial holidays even the poorest of the poor would make their best effort to have something new to wear for church, even though it was homemade, and they would go to church together as a family.

Vasilis remembers very little of the religious home life of the family; with the exception that always belief in God, honesty, integrity, character and truthfulness, no matter what the cost, was stressed in the family. His mother would say, "The liar and the thief rejoice only the first year." By this she implied that the second year they would be caught. There were times that the Paterumon or the Lord's Prayer was recited before the meal.

Vasilis' mother was the storyteller of the family. Quite often they would sit around the fireplace and she would share stories of the saints and she always drew a moral lesson out of it for the children. Most of the stories were influenced from the tradition of the Greek Orthodox Church, and the children were taught to pray to the Virgin Mary and to the saints. They made promises or bargained with the saints that if their prayer was answered, they would light a candle to their honor or do something else.

Since the only means of transportation was by foot, horseback or donkeys, there was always time and opportunity for social interaction and the development of strong relationships beyond the family circle. There was interdependence on each other in the whole community. The great high moments of cooperation came during harvesting; shearing the sheep, the thrashing of the wheat, the gathering of grapes and the clearing a path in the snow during the winter so the villagers could reach the church, the vrisi, and the kids could make it to the school.

The most memorable times were the summer evenings where the adults would gather together in each neighborhood for conversation while kids filled the air with laughter playing with their homemade toys and playing hide and seek. There was no one in the village that faced any need, sorrow or loss alone. The whole village came to the rescue of each other no matter what the problem.

The celebration of several holidays would bring the villagers together for outstanding meals, lively entertainment with the mbouzouki and the clarinet and the engagement of friendly competition. For example during the epiphany, the priest would throw a small cross in the water and the men dove in to retrieve it. He who was successful always received a prize. The celebration of the saint Elias, Elijah, was a big thing in the community. One or two miles from the village there was a church built on the top of the hill in honor of the saint Elijah and the men would have a race from the village to that church and back and the winner would receive a loaf of bread in which there were hidden silver coins.

One of the things that is uncommon in a lot of places, especially in our days, was very common in that village in those days. It appeared that everyone had the right to both correct and help the children. They were the most precious commodity of the village.

Vasilis remembers very little of his first seven formative years. He remembers his only boyhood friend George Rounis, whom he met lately in Greece and has renewed correspondence. George was heartbroken when Vasilis moved away during the civil war in 1946. Then they had a small encounter in the close of the 1950s and the beginning of the 1960s in Athens. George went on to Paris for studies, became a lawyer and then worked for the European Common Market in Brussels for 25 or 30 years. He is now retired in Greece and spends his time between Athens and the village. Another friend is George Paraskevopoulos, the only one that Vasilis remembers who went in the first grade with him.

George never left the village that Vasilis knows of, but while in the village he was elected mayor for a period of time. Vasilis got reacquainted with him in the summer of 2009.

There are some weak memories in Vasilis' mind about his school experience in the first grade in the village school. It was a one room school with a wooden stove in the back of the room to keep the room warm during the winter months. He recalls during breaks the kids gathered around the stove to keep themselves warm. Since most of the kids were older than the normal school age, the older ones would intimidate the younger ones and would not allow them to get close to the stove. Quite often there were fights among the students around the stove which frightened Vasilis and did not give him a positive feeling

Vasilis with his childhood friend George Rounis, Thanasis and Yeota

toward the school. The teacher in that school was always a male and very strong in discipline. For punishment quite often he would put the bigger kids to stand at the corner on one foot while holding both hands up in the air with some kind of weight in them. Such an experience had a mixed message for Vasilis as far as education was concerned.

Some of the delightful memories of his early childhood were watching the lambs grazing in the family

Vasilis with his first grade schoolmate, George Paraskevopoulos

field next to the house, walking in the creek which led to the vrisi and gathering juicy blackberries on either side of the creek. There were times that he endeavored to climb the sycomouria, a tree which was a cross between a fig tree and a berry tree, producing large, long berries. There were times that he was scolded for reaching for some cherries from trees whose branches were almost covering the path that he was traveling. Since shoes were a rare commodity, he spent a lot of time trying to get thorns out of his feet and cried a lot when his toes would get stumped on a rock. But he recalls that his childhood was both secure and happy in spite of the hardships and the uncertain circumstances of life. Come Christmas time he was going to receive a pair of house shoes being made by his mother from sheep wool.

LIFE-THREATENING ENCOUNTERS AND PROVIDENTIAL ANGELS

Vasilis at 17 years old

"For my people have committed two evils; they have forsaken me the fountain of living waters, and hewed them out cisterns, broken cisterns, that can hold no water"

Jeremiah 2:13.

"And David longed, and said, Oh that one would give me drink of the water of the well of Bethlehem, which is by the gate!"

As Vasilis was entering his third birthday and he was able to converse and explore his surroundings and getting familiar with the house. He had no awareness what was awaiting his country, the serenity of his small village and the dangers that were about to engulf his family and his own life. Neither he nor his family had any idea how divine providence was going to hover over them with protection and in making a way of escape.   There was no way the family could have envisioned what was going to happen to the country, the storms that were about to begin raging and beat on the family, nor of the impact that it was going to have on each member of the family.

In October 1940 there was a big celebration in Athens where the tables were decorated with Greek and Italian flags (some call the Greeks and the Italians first cousins!), and a big banner was hanged up which said, "Long Live Greece".   The royal family and the prime minister, Ioannis Metaxas were expected to attend the opera.   But at three o'clock on the morning of October 28, Grazzi, the Italian ambassador to Greece awakened Metaxas with a message from Mussolini, demanding that the Italian troops be allowed to occupy the country. Metaxas replied in French, "Alozs, c'est la querra." Popular legend has condensed Metaxas' reply into one word, "Ochi" – "No"; which has become the battle cry of the Greeks. Every 28th of October signs and banners bloom defiantly on the walls throughout Greece with this battle cry.   Mussolini had given Metaxas three hours to respond, but his troops had already begun to cross from the Albanian border into Greece.[1]

Outnumbered two to one, the Greeks astonished the Italian generals with their courage and the accuracy of their artillery; although they had only six mortars for each division against the invaders 60. The early and bitter cold winter fought on the Greek side, a lot of Italians became victims of "white death" (a swelling of the feet which looked like potatoes and then it would burst open). In the end 12,368 Italians returned home mutilated by frostbite, 13,755 were buried in the mud of Greece, and another 25,067 were missing. Within a month the Greeks had driven the invaders into Albania and further. By December they had taken the port of Aghies Sarantes, which had been renamed by the Italians, Edita, in honor of Mussolini's daughter.

The entire western world was deeply surprised and took hope from the incredible Greek victory. The Greeks were moved with pride and patriotism and they began to cry, "On to Rome". But their joy did not last long, as we shall see later.[2]

Vasilis, his family and the peace-loving inhabitants of this remote village, were practically unaware of all the happenings in Northern Greece. The delayed stories came through travelers the Greeks had defeated the Italians. Vasilis' growth, even though in its early stages, began to reveal some of his personal traits of being curious, inquisitive, determined and having difficulty accepting the word "no" for an answer to his request. It was his unyielding determination that sometimes led him to dangerous situations even when he was very young, to the extent that his life was threatened. But his escape from some things is not short of miraculous or divine intervention. Some would call it luck, but we call it divine protection.

When Vasilis was a little more than three years old, one evening his father came home after he had traveled to another village, and after the evening meal while sitting around the fireplace told the family the following story. An 8-year-old boy in the village had taken some pills and died. The common medicine that was prescribed in those days was some sugarcoated pink pills called kinino which were prescribed for almost anything. Once the sugar coating was gone, the pills were very bitter. The father had warned the family to keep the medicine out of the reach of children. But was there any one who could keep anything out of the reach of Vasilis?

The next day while the family had gone to work in the fields, the only two that remained in the house were Vasilis and his grandmother. While the grandmother was sitting on the porch conversing with the neighbors, Vasilis began to explore the house. His curiosity led him to the kitchen table which had a drawer, but it was too tall for Vasilis to reach it. But his curiosity and determination to find out what was in the drawer did not keep him away for too long. He gathered as many pillows as he could find, put them on the top of each other and soon he had achieved his goal. He had opened the table drawer. His explorative curiosity continued until he discovered a small bottle full of pink pills, between 8 and 12 of them. In some way he managed to open the bottle and after he tasted the sweetness of the first pill, he proceeded to swallow all of them. Then he ran outside on the porch where his grandmother was sitting with the neighbors and said to her in Greek, "Yiayia, kita, eurika mia mboukalitsa – Grandmom, look, I found a little bottle." To which the grandmother replied with a panic in her voice, "Paidakimou, my child, what did you do with the pills that were in the bottle?" His response, "Ta efaga, yiayia – I ate them, grandma." At that time the grandmother panicked and began to cry out in Greek, "To paidi epire to kinino kai tha pethani – the child has taken the pills and he is going to die."

Her voice was so filled with panic that the whole neighborhood gathered at the house and every one had some kind of remedy on how to save Vasilis' life. There were two neighbor ladies who took strong initiative and who were confident that they were doing the right thing. Vasilis calls them his providential angels even though their names are forgotten. One of the ladies forced Vasilis to drink vinegar out of a bottle and the other lady continued to feed him honey with a teaspoon. The process continued for a few moments, and it appeared cruel to treat a child that way. We have no way of knowing if the ladies knew of the effects that their treatment would have on Vasilis. But later it was confirmed that vinegar works to dissolve the poison, while the honey was coating the stomach and keeping it from absorbing it. By the time the family came home from the fields, Vasilis was in a coma and the family and neighbors had a longer than 24 hour vigil awaiting the outcome. We lack a lot of details as to what else took place during those tense hours. But after 30 hours or so, Vasilis suddenly woke up as if nothing had taken place and he called out to a cousin of his that lived next door, "Stavroula, look at me, I was dead but now I am alive again."

Both the family and the neighbors thought Vasilis' recovery was a miracle and his mother did not cease to thank God in the best way she knew how. The incident came and went and a lot of things have been forgotten, but there was a mark that never left Vasilis. It was the nickname that they gave him, Mboukalitsa, little bottle. The good thing is that it remained in the village and it never followed Vasilis anywhere else. Even to this day the older people, who remember the story, address him as Mboukalitsa when he visits the village of his birth.

Quite often it was Vasilis' own determination and his unwillingness to accept counsel that led him to some dangerous predicaments which are too numerous to mention here. It was a summer day after the harvest of the wheat had taken place and the sheaves of the wheat had been brought to the threshing place called aloni. Now the aloni was a round place whose floor was level and hard, giving the appearance of cement even though it was made from clay. From its center it was ten meters around. There was a post placed in the middle. Workers spread the wheat sheaves on the threshing floor and then brought five to six horses yoked all together on a straight line, then a rope with a loop would go around the post and as the horses marched around and around, their feet threshed the wheat.

Vasilis was about five at the time and was very fascinated by the process. Work had begun a little past 10:30 in the morning. There were about five family members engaged in the process and possibly two neighbors. Within thirty minutes into the process, Vasilis began to aggravate his parents that he was hungry. Even though they advised him that it was about an hour to noontime and they were going to have lunch, he insisted he wanted to eat right then. The result, he spent some time crying, which was not unusual for him. About noon they announced it was time for lunch and everybody was going to the house to eat. One person would stay behind to make sure the horses continued the threshing process, and that they were not allowed to eat the wheat. Vasilis decided he did not want to eat then, but stay at the aloni with his mother and help with the horses. He persuaded his mother to allow him to enter in the aloni with the switch and make sure the horses were going faster. When a neighbor stopped by for a visit, his mother yielded to his demands and allowed him to get in the aloni. As he got close and used the switch on the horses, one of the horses kicked him close to his spleen and knocked him flat to the ground unconscious. If the neighbor were not there to jump in and pull him out, the horses would have trampled over him. They rushed him to the priest of the town who had served as a paramedic in the army and now was acting as a doctor because there was no doctors anywhere close by. The priest said the horse kick missed Vasilis' spleen by a hair and that he was not sure if any of his internal organs were damaged; only time would tell. Again Vasilis says God had placed His providential angel in the right place at the right time to save his life.

Someone has said, "Be careful what you want because you might get it." It was Vasilis' persistence and determination to get what he wanted, when he wanted, that led him to some dangerous problems. It was in the middle of July or so when Vasilis and his oldest brother were in the house and from the window were watching their flock which was grazing in their field. Below the field was divided in the middle by a small creek. Around the property there was a stone fence but it was not tall enough to keep the sheep from moving to the neighbor's field. On the farthest part of the land from the house there were a couple pear trees that belonged to the neighbor but half of their branches were leaning toward Vasilis' family property.

For about thirty minutes Vasilis aggravated his oldest brother to allow him to go and turn the sheep around because they were getting too close to the neighbor's property. But Vasilis' concern was not so much on what the sheep were going to do; he had his eyes on the pear trees. He wanted to get some pears.

Finally his brother gave in and allowed Vasilis to go. He pretended to be turning the sheep around and then he ran for the pear trees. Quickly he filled his shirt with pears that made him look like a pregnant woman. As he began to run from fear that someone might see him, he slipped as he was crossing the creek, fell down and a stick entered his right eye close to his nose. Vasilis began to scream as blood had covered his face and from the fear that now his brother was going to catch him with the evidence of the crime. He was too young and unaware to know that the scripture says, "Be sure your sin will find you out" and it did.

His brother Thanasis ran to his aid and took him to the village's paramedic; the priest. He packed his eye with some gauze and said, "Now, we have to wait and see what damage has been done and if his eye could be saved." But miraculously the injury did not have any lasting effects on Vasilis' eye, but it did not cure him or curtail his mischievousness.

It is not our intent here to expose all the mischievousness and the childhood foolishness, but any time he came home with something that was not his, he told his mother he had founded it. His mother politely told him to go and put it back where he had founded it, because normally it was from the yard of one of the neighbors.

When Vasilis was about six years old or so, he and his only and best friend George Rounis were inseparable. They played and did everything together and seemingly they never

The Greeks' joy of repelling and defeating the Italians was short-lived. The news arrived that Hitler had given Greece the same ultimatum, surrender or war. Metaxas again replied to the Germans with the same emphatic "Ochi" – No, that he had replied to the Italians. His response infuriated Hitler and on April 6, 1941, Hitler with his elite army attacked Greece from the Bulgarian border and within days every Greek plane was destroyed and there appeared that there was no hope for resistance.

Greece had entered its biggest nightmare ever. For three years terror, fear, pain, suffering, separation and torture combined with death, reigned throughout the country. Whole villages went up in smoke and flames. Whole families were totally erased from existence. Greece was covered as if it was a black blanket with the song of mourning. It was miriology, the song of mourning coming from the flute of the shepherds covering the hillsides of Greece. It replaced the operas in the cities. Even though some villages were turned into dust, most villages fared better than the big cities. But it was in the villages that one saw the visible pain and anguish. Mothers and daughters, wives and sisters, all dressed in black and the miriology, the song of mourning, would be heard in every location and at every hour of the day.

On April 27, 1941, the Germans entered the deserted streets of Athens, the capital of Greece, and raised their flag on Acropolis, Greece's most historical landmark. King George and the government escaped to Crete. News of the war was hard to come by. The government had collapsed. The currency was worthless and it appeared that each man and family were out for themselves. There were no telephone services or even radios in order to get the news. Only those who had escaped shared what they had seen and experienced as they passed from town to town searching for a safe place.

It is not quite clear as to when the news about the war reached Vasilis' village. As the church bells began to ring villagers gathered in the main village square, instructions were given of routes to follow for escaping and places to hide. Watchmen were appointed to inform the villagers of the approaching Germans and direct their escape routes. The stories of horror shared by those who had escaped spread fear and panic. No one wanted to stay behind and face the Germans. Families gathered the mere necessities for survival, loaded their donkey or mule and they were ready to escape to the mountains. Each individual was assigned a responsibility, including small children. Vasilis was assigned to carry a specially prepared goat's skin which contained feta cheese mixed with salty milk for preservation.

Mr. Nicholas Gage states in his book, Eleni, that in the winter of 1941-1942, because all the routes of supply were cut off, "Athens became a nightmare of skeletal figures with bellies swollen, shuffling hopelessly in reach for food, falling dead and lay unburied in the streets. The children and the elderly died first. On the first two months of that winter 300,000 died in the capital.[1]

As the occupying Germans spread like a blanket covering Greece, there were a few cat and mouse scrimmages by some Greeks which infuriated the Germans. In any village or town where a German was killed, it was guaranteed the next day that village or town would go up in flames and any man captured would be executed. The Germans entered several times in Vasilis' village called Agridion, but they almost always found it empty. The exception was when sometimes the elderly who were not able to travel to the mountains refused to go and stayed behind. At one occasion as the Germans approaching the village they were attacked by the Antartes and seven or eight of them were killed. The next day, as a reprisal, the Germans returned to the village in fury and vengeance to inflict pain and destruction. Several men who were found in the village were executed and one was hanged in the village square and set some of the main buildings on fire.

55

On another occasion, Vasilis' grandmother was not well and she refused to travel to the mountain. She said, "I am going to stay in my house and if I die, I die." Then when the whole ordeal was over, and the family returned back home she would recount her experience. "They were just young boys. They would enter the house, search everything and what they found would put it in the center of the floor and destroy it." Bamboo spools which the ladies used for weaving, they would throw them on the floor and step on them. Bags full of wheat which was hidden, were taken to the street, cut open with their sword and the wheat was spread on the ground. It was not unusual upon returning from the mountains to find everything destroyed and the house burned. There were times that they would torture the elderly who had stayed behind in order to tell them where the villagers were hiding, and at times they killed some of them.

The Germans did not have a good experience in the mountains. Therefore they were reluctant to venture toward them, especially when the passage was very narrow. It was in places like these that they suffered their worst defeats. Vasilis recalls some of the things as they observed from the distance of the mountains the movements of the Germans. When they approached a narrow place, always they sent a dog first, then in distance would follow a single soldier, then two and two more and if it had proven safe the rest would follow.

There was a time, sometime in the beginning of 1944, where a heated battle took place in the town of Glogova, near Vasilis' village of Agridion. The battle raged for days and young Vasilis thought the earth was shaken and the world was coming to an end. It was in that battle where the Germans and the Italians were defeated.

Some of the Germans and Italians who were escaping for their lives were heading toward Vasilis' village. The watchmen advised the villagers accordingly and the men of the village took after them with sticks and stones. Vasilis' cousin tells the story that when the villagers surrounded some of them, one of the Italian soldiers fell on his knees and raised both hands up crying in a loud voice, "Picula, picula, children, children." Meaning that he had little children back home and he was begging for his life. War is an ugly thing and it expresses itself in barbarous acts. The conclusion of this story should move even the coldest heart to reflect and call for compassion.

Vasilis' family, with the exception of his grandmother, never came face to face with the Germans. Their observations always were from a distance. The exoduses from the village were frequent, but there were times that there were false alarms. In one occasion of such exodus, after walking for a long time the villagers arrived close to a high mountain where a river was formed. They gathered in a flat area to pass the rest of the day and the night. As everyone was preparing to settle down, the watchmen announced that the Germans had begun to move upwards in the river toward their direction. Pandemonium hit the camp. In all the confusion, someone had some chickens and a rooster which without warning began to crow. Vasilis witnessed the immediate execution of the rooster on the chopping block without a trial because it had betrayed their hiding place. As they began to move the opposite direction of the Germans' movement, immediately they were informed by the watchmen that it was a false alarm.

There were 150 villages that were completely burned down. But the atrocity of the war and its pain are epitomized in what happened in a small town called Kalivrita, near the city of Patra. There were 2,500 inhabitants thought there was nothing to fear. One day the church bells called the people to the town square at 6:00 p.m. They were divided into two groups, women and children under twelve years old and men and boys over twelve years old. The women and the children were taken to the schoolhouse, and they were locked in. The 800 men and boys were taken some yards away, close to the town cemetery and after watching their town set on fire they were cut down with machine guns. Then the school was set on fire which caused the women to begin breaking windows and throwing their children out for survival. One of the German soldiers took pity on them, he opened the school door and some of the women were able to escape.[2]

What happened in Kalivrita became the battle cry of Greece. Songs of mourning were heard everywhere. Vasilis had heard the stories of horror, the songs that had been written about the town and its people and always wanted to walk in that place, meet some of the survivors and hear their story. In June of 2009, he had the opportunity to visit this historic town. The town is rebuilt and it is more beautiful than ever, but the monuments erected in the execution area serve as a sad reminder of the ugliness of war. As he walked around the monuments, read the hundreds of names engraved on them (more than 50 were under 19 years old), sorrow like a dark blanket covered his soul and it was difficult to hold back tears.

There was a certain sobriety and reverence that gripped his soul as he looked at the words on the ground in white letters, Ochi polemo, ala eireni, -- "No more war, but Peace." Then Vasilis went into the center of the town where there were souvenir shops and cafenois, cafes. Could there be someone here who had witnessed all those atrocities of the war? He made his way into one of the souvenir shops that was tended by an 84-year-old lady dressed in black. Her face was wrinkled but there was a spark in her eyes and springs on her feet. All the things in the shop were handmade by the people of the town and Vasilis bought two coffee cups.

After his purchase, Vasilis engaged the lady in conversation by asking questions that had been brewing within him for years. He asked her if she had any knowledge of the things that took place during the war in her town. There was a serious sadness that covered her face and then looking up straight in the eyes of Vasilis she said in Greek, "Paidakimou, eimai mia apo tois gunekes pou etreksan ekso apo tin fotia tou scholeiou" – My child, I am one of the women who escaped from the burning school. Vasilis froze on his feet. Her story confirmed all that he had heard, read and more. There is no need here to share more information because it is not our main purpose to write about the atrocities of the war, but all these shaped Vasilis' life and they had an impact on his views.

The family of Vasilis did not have any face to face encounters with the Germans or the Italians, except his grandmother who decided to remain in the village during some of the exoduses. The thing that we failed to share though is that Vasilis' oldest brother, Thanasis, had gone to Douneka, a town in Southern Peloponnesus, where he was employed as a shepherd boy in 1942-1943. He had encounters with the Germans and the scars to prove it remain. Thanasis got sick with high fever with no help coming from anywhere. Somehow some German paramedic saw him and had pity on him. They treated him by giving him some pills and in a couple days he got better. He always shares the experience with deep appreciation and gratitude.

One of the most devastating weapons of the war is land mines. A lot of innocent people were killed by land mines even after the war was over. Thanasis was involved in a land mine accident which caused him the loss of one of his eyes and left him with some scars.

The war ended in the late 1944 and early 1945. Nicholas Gage says when the British landed in Piraeus and then entered Athens, the population responded with celebrations. One observer notes, "For three days and nights, hungry, sick people spitting blood marched without sleeping, kept going by a collective delirium, the joy of new found freedom."[3]

1. Nicholas Gage, Eleni, Ballantine Books, New York 1983, pp. 65-67.

2. Nicholas Gage, <u>Eleni</u>, Ballantine Books, New York 1983, pp.148-149.

3. Nicholas Gage, <u>Eleni</u>, Ballantine Books, New York 1983, pp.174-175.

THE DEVASTATION OF DEPRESSION
AND SUSTAINING GRACE

Vasilis kneeling, his cousin Dyonisis, his sister Yeota, his mother, his cousin Vaso and his brother Thanasis

"For I was an hungred,   and you gave me no meat: I was thirsty, and ye gave me no drink: I was a stranger, and ye took me not in: naked, and ye clothed me not: sick, and in prison, and ye visited me not"

(Matthew 25:42-43).

By December of 1941 Greece was occupied by two foreign powers, the Germans and the Italians. Even though there were a few pockets of resistance both from the left and the right, the enemy began to enter in every town and village with the vengeance of destruction. There were only a few villages that escaped the constant occupation of the enemy, which lasted more than three years. The main routes of supply were interrupted and the fate of the majority of the people was not determined only by the will and the sword of the enemy, but also by the sword of hunger. Hunger began spreading itself over Greece as a dark blanket and its cry echoed from the mountains to the valleys, from the villages to the crowded cities, bringing a trail of fear, terror and open graves. It is not certain that anyone knows for sure how many people died from starvation in Greece during those three years, except that which has been reported for Athens in the three months of the winter of 1941-1942, which claimed 300,000 lives.

Since lines of communication and travel were almost nonexistent, most of the people were ignorant concerning the state of things around the country and the suffering that was engulfing young and old alike. The depression was more devastating in the cities because there was absolutely nothing that could contribute to the survival of the people. And if it were not for the Marshal Plan, as it was stated earlier, Greece would have become a mass grave with no epitaph. The chance of survival in the villages was better than that in the city. There was something that the people could glean from the land and most of the people in the villages would have some livestock, sheep, goats and chickens. Vasilis recalls unending lines of people going from door to door and from town to town with small bags in their hands begging for anything that could contribute to their survival.

Vasilis' family did not escape the agony and the effects of the depression. It proved to be costly to them. They worked hard and they invented methods of ingenuity which did not deliver them from the pain and hardship of the depression but contributed to their survival. There were times the lack of necessities was so severe that there was nothing to satisfy the pangs of hunger. Vasilis would sit in the middle of the floor and would cry to the top of his voice, "I am hungry" for a long time without any response or satisfaction to his cry, with the exception of the kiss and the comforting words of his mother.

The first step for survival was taken by Vasilis' father who sent his oldest son, Thanasis, to the town of Douneka in the southern part of Peloponnesus to take care of the flock of a well-to-do person. He was barely 13 years old. But it was certain that he would have something to eat and shelter. It is not clear whether he was paid anything else. The two years that he spent there were filled with hardship, loneliness, and suffering and of course, pain from the accident that cost him his eye. But his patience, positive attitude, hard work and loyalty paid off to a certain extent and he later became the sole initiator for the survival of the family.

Christos, the other brother of Vasilis, who was 10 years old at that time, was put in charge of the few goats and sheep which the family shared with a relative in the village. The relative was the priest of the village, in a place called Calivia some distance from the village. There he was left practically alone while from time to time his mother or father would make the 45 minute trip there, and bring him whatever they had which could be helpful. His mother would always crochet house shoes from wool which were soled with pigskin to protect his feet from the elements. Some time ago Vasilis asked Christos about those times, because he could not remember anything personally. Christos began to share with him in an emotional way and with tears, describing the fears and the hunger, the loneliness and the pain that he experienced during that time. He talked about the thorns on his feet, the fear as darkness covered the place at night and his emotional outcry when his mother and dad would visit him and he did not want them to leave.

He shared with Vasilis one of his most frightening and humorous experiences of that time. His mother had made him a beautiful pair of shoes from wool and had sewed pigskin underneath. He was both proud and protective of them because they provided comfort for his feet. But on a beautiful summer day as he was tending the flock in the field, he sat under the shade of a tree to rest and fell asleep. When he awoke the flock was nowhere to be seen and as he began to run in search of the flock, he noticed that one of his shoes was missing from his foot as the thorns were finding their way into his foot. He panicked. He thought a dog had come while he was sleeping and took his shoe away. He started to cry and looking for his shoe to no avail. He began to run in search of the flock and in crying saying at the same time, "They will kill me, not only I lost my shoe but I lost the sheep also." His heart was beating fast, his feet hurting from the thorns, tears running down his cheeks, and with a lump in his throat, he continued the search for his sheep and goats. Finally when he found them his fears subsided, dried up his tears and brought a smile to his face when he realized that the missing shoe was in his hands all this time!

Vasilis' mother and dad would go to the mountain side of the village and they would gather wild vegetables and wild pears by the bushels. They would split the wild pears in four, remove the core and the seeds and then spread them out in the sun to dry. When dried, they would take them to the water mill and make flour out of them. It was almost like a chocolate cake mix, but very sticky when it was baked as bread. They would do anything within their power for the survival of the family. In spite of the hardship they were not selfish and always noticed people whose fate was worse than theirs. When people came to their door begging with their small bags, Vasilis' dad would dip with a bowl in the barrel where they had stored the wild pear flour, would fill it up and empty it in the bag of the people. Quite often Vasilis' mother would admonish his dad by saying concerning his giving, "Dino, take it easy, we have children and we do not know what is going to happen tomorrow." But it did not make much difference to him, he continued his practice and when the words were repeated from the mother again, his response was always the same, "The Lord will provide", and He did provide.

Vasilis recalls both with wonder and amusement that wheat flour at that time was a rare thing in the village. But after that incident every so often the family would find close to the back door of the house a small bag with a couple pounds of wheat flour. It happened more than twice. Was this a response to the faith of the father who had said, "The Lord will provide"? Vasilis thinks that it was. The wonderful thing was that when you mix the pear flour with the wheat flour, you had something tasty, almost like a chocolate cake.

Vasilis' father found other avenues which contributed to the survival of the family. He would load his donkey with four large bags of wild pear flour and he would make the two day trip to the southern part of Peloponnesus where they produce a lot of vegetables, oranges, lemons, resin and olive oil. He traded the flour for olive oil that was a savior for the family. Other times he would take a tool with him that was seasonable for labor and make the two-day trip, work for two weeks and then load himself with whatever necessities he could secure and he would go back to the family.

Vasilis recalls at one time things were so bad there was nothing to eat and someone gave his mother the cobs of the corn without the corn. They got the idea that they could ground them, make flour, and then make corn bread with it. They mixed it with water and whatever else you put to make bread and they put it outside in the clay oven to bake. On the due time when the mother went to check on it, the water had evaporated and it had caught on fire. The kids laughed and used it as what they call in Greek fotobolides, flares.

During that time Vasilis' mother assumed more responsibility for the support of the family. She would go and work in the fields for people from sunrise to sunset. Sometimes the employer would provide lunch for the employees, which consisted of a piece of bread, and possibly a piece of feta cheese. She would never eat the piece of bread but took it home so she could divide it equally with all the members of the family.

There were times that Vasilis and his sister Yeota would visit his Godfather and Godmother. They were well off people who would treat them with some of the things they did not have at home. At one time they gave them a slice of wheat bread and his sister refused to allow Vasilis to take a bite. She watched him all the way home to make sure the bread arrived untouched and that everyone in the family had a chance to have a small piece.

Even though the depression experience had devastating effects on Vasilis and his family, and even though they were scattered in four different directions, and the prolonged separation caused untold suffering and pain, at the end it had developed such strong interdependence for the family and prepared it for that which was about to follow that they had never envisioned.

As the end of the war was approaching (even though the family was not aware) the family began to pull together. Once again all the family members were together in their humble dwelling. They began to cultivate their fields and vineyards and tend their flock. It appeared the sun of hope was rising again and their spirits were lifted with a new vision of optimism and anticipation. The God who had demonstrated His faithfulness in sustaining them through the war and depression would be the same God who would guide them in the future no matter how uncertain it might prove to be.

It was the firm belief of the family, especially projected through the mother and her disposition, that God was with them and that He was not going to forsake them. He who sent manna from heaven to sustain the people of Israel in the wilderness, He was the same God who sent a bag with a couple pounds of flour to Vasilis' door to sustain the family. Rightly the hymn writer exhorts us to look at the faithfulness of God. [1]

1. Barney E. Warner, "The Faithfulness of God", *Worship the Lord, Hymnal of the Church of God*, Warner Press, Anderson, Indiana, 1989, No. 651

THE CIVIL WAR, ITS PAIN, LOSS
AND LASTING EFFECTS

Vasilis' Dad with his portable store!

"Therefore is the anger of the lord kindled against his people, and he hath stretched forth his hand against them, and hath smitten them; and the hills did tremble, and their carcasses were torn in the midst of the streets"

Isaiah 5:25.

"When buffalo battle in the march, it's the frogs that pay."
Greek Proverb

.

By the fall of 1942 the war and the depression had affected every family in Greece. There was no one who had not suffered some kind of loss and pain. Families were mourning the loss of their loved ones and most of the women were dressed in black, the sign of mourning. The pain was more intense for some people because it was not inflicted by the Germans or the depression, but by their own people, Greeks who collaborated with the Germans and used their position to settle individual scores with people that they did not like for one reason or another. People had become paranoid, did not know whom to trust and when that midnight knock would come at their door and cause their loved one to disappear and never be seen again.

The family of Vasilis had begun to adjust to the circumstances which surrounded them and they had learned to cope both with the war and the depression. It appeared that their safety was guaranteed, but they were not aware of the noticeable rumblings and the group dynamics that had come to a boiling point and were ready, like a volcano, to erupt. No one could envision that the darkest days for Greece and Vasilis' family were ahead. Neither were the common people aware that there were powers outside Greece that were playing checkers with its destiny. In fact, a great deal of the future of Greece was determined by those outside of Greece.

In June of 1942 in a small village called Dominitso, 185 miles northwest of Athens, appeared a man named Aris with 14 other uniformed individuals. He announced he was raising a revolt against the occupying forces and called his group, The Greek Popular Liberation Army, which was going to be known by the Greek initials, Ellas. They were going to be known as antartes or guerillas and eventually were going to have the support of Communist Bloc.

On July 23, 1942, a fellow with the name Napoleon Zervas, who did not fit the profile of a guerrilla (if Vasilis is not mistaken his roots were in aristocracy), left Athens for the mountains of his native Epiros in order to form resistance group, and because of his ideology he named it Edes, the initials of National Democratic League.

In early 1944 before the British landed at Piraeus, the Germans had sensed that they were losing the war. Therefore, they began to unleash a wave of vicious reprisals. In the village Destino, near Delphi, 228 individuals were murdered, including 20 children under the age of five. Some of the northern cities of Greece had large Jewish communities which is said that in 1942 the Germans gathered 46,000 Jews in Salonika (Thessaloniki) and shipped them to the German consecration camps.

The resistance groups gained momentum and Ellas controlled more territory than Edes with the arrival of the British and the defeat of the Germans. The Allies had occupied Greece and their task now was to deal with the two opposing fronts, Ellas and Edes. In fact on December 3, 1944, Ellas decided to stage a coup in Athens and attacked both the British and the Greek troops and they searched from door to door for real and imaginary enemies, executing 13,500 people in three weeks.

It is not our aim here to fully describe the civil war of Greece, but to give a bird 's eye view of the war and the effects it had on Vasilis and his family. The civil war had three rounds and the third and last one was the bloodiest and the most costly for every Greek family. There were agreements signed and deals worked out between Stalin and Churchill. Promises were made to Ellas that it would participate in the future government of Greece, therefore they should surrender their arms. Some were suspicious and did not trust anyone. A great number of the Ellas group fled into the Communist Bloc countries such as Albania, Bulgaria and Yugoslavia. But coming close to election time, they felt that the promises made to them were not kept, so they boycotted the election and began to attack places in the north. That started the most vicious civil war, Greeks against Greeks, the one calling the others traitors and they endeavored to settle real or imaginary scores. It was at this point that Vasilis' family began to be engulfed in the viciousness of the war.

Vasilis had a first cousin who was a freedom fighter with the resistance group called Ellas. Their ideology was that of Communism. Even though they were fighting to liberate the country, their aim was to set up a government that would support their ideology. He achieved some military ranking in Ellas and in the early part of the third round of the war, he was captured. Due to the fact that he remained unrepented and defiant, he was court-martialed and executed. Because of that relationship and due to the fact that Vasilis' family was bearing the same last name, the family was marked by the right that they might be collaborating with the freedom fighters.

Vasilis' father was hired by someone, together with several others from the village with their mules, in order to transport some wooden boxes from a neighboring place to a secret place close to the village. It turned out the wooden boxes contained guns and ammunition, but we are not sure whether the transporters knew. But someone reported it to the authorities. So the next evening, at midnight, all those gentlemen, including Vasilis' father received that dreadful knock at the door, and they carried him away in the darkness of the night. They were taken into an undisclosed location, beaten and interrogated. Since the men had been sworn to secrecy, in the beginning they refused to give any information. The beating broke down weak wills and one after another they began to confess with the exception of Vasilis' father. He was a man of his word and nothing was going to make him go back on his word. He was beaten repeatedly to the extent that he had turned black and blue, but he refused to share any information while all others had done so. Finally when he heard all others had confessed, he admitted his involvement.

He was thrown in jail without a trial for 18 months. The jail was a long distance by foot from the village. When finally the family learned exactly where he was held, Vasilis' mother made the long and painful trip to visit him, but when she saw him, he was beaten so badly that she did not even recognize him. None of the other members of the family were able to visit him. They saw him only after 18 months when he was released. Nine times they had set a time for trial and nine times it was postponed. His poor wife made the trip all these times but her hopes always ended in disappointment.

Vasilis' brother, Christos, was about 13 years old at that time and had the full responsibility of taking care of the flock. There were many times that he did without food and other necessities while his mother was making those long trips to the jail. Someone who did not like the family and wanted to pay it back in vengeance, went to the police and told them that Christos, while he was grazing his flock, was meeting with the antartes, passing information to them and supplies. Of course all these were lies, but the political climate was such that a person in position of power could do anything and get by with it. The police went where Christos was tending his flock and they took him away, without the knowledge of the family, to the police station in another town, quite a distance away. They subjected this 13-year-old to the most unbearable beating and torture in order to confess. There was nothing to confess. They used on him a torture called Falanga in Greek, where they take your shoes off, interlock your feet with the belt of the rifle to the extent that you cannot move your feet and then with another rifle they beat the soles of your feet. The pain is excruciating. Soon your feet swell, break out and bleed. It is impossible to stand on them, walk or put anything on them. Day in and day out, the beating continued with the promise that when he would confess, it would stop. But he was telling the truth, he had not seen any antartes and he had not given any supplies to anyone; he did not have enough to survive himself.

When the beating became so unbearable and he could stand it no longer, in order to avoid it, he decided to lie and say "Yes" to everything that they asked. "Did you see the antartes?" "Yes" was his reply. "Did you see so and so with them?" Again, the reply was "Yes". So they began to bring the individuals in, whose names he had mentioned that they had been seen with the antartes. One day they brought in the respectable gentleman of the town and asked Christos, "Was he with the antartes?" Christos without blinking an eye said, "He was." Then the gentleman approached Christos and with a soft and rather compassionate voice asked him, "Son, did you really see me with the antartes?" Christos replied, "Yes, you were there, were you not?"

When the interrogation had ended, the gentleman asked to see the chief of police and he said to him, "You ought to be ashamed for torturing an innocent young boy. Can you not see that in order to avoid the pain he will tell you anything that you want to hear?" After that he was not beaten anymore and he was not locked up, but had freedom to move around the police station. But still they kept him for three months. Later when things changed and Christos met the gentleman who had lied against him and had caused him all that suffering, he was a gentleman and he did not allow hate to remain in his heart.

The events which had transpired in Vasilis' family caused his older brother Thanasis to go to the police station to intercede for his brother, but he was detained and threatened with imprisonment. He was let go later with the full realization that the threat to the family was real and he was not sure it could survive under the present circumstances. War, depression and imprisonment were taking their toll and signs of desperation began to appear on the horizon. Vasilis' mother worked like a slave to provide and keep the family together. Thanasis, the oldest brother, in the absence of the father, began to assume the leadership role of the man of the house.

It was during those difficult days that appeals were made to Greek patriots who lived in the United States of America to send aid to their families so that Greece could survive. Vasilis' mother had a brother who had immigrated to Salt Lake City, Utah, either in 1912 or 1918, but communication was a rare thing. When he heard the news about the suffering in Greece, he decided to send a horse to his sister to use it to plow the fields and for any other helpful way. It took three or four months for the horse to arrive in Greece by boat. When it arrived there, not only was it wild and no one could approach it, but it almost had starved to death. It was skin and bones; besides it could not understand Greek! What was supposed to have been a help to the family turned out to become a nightmare. Vasilis has no recollection how they got the horse to the village. Everyone in the village came to see the big horse that came from America, but no one could get close to it and no one could do anything with it. Additionally they discovered they did not have enough of anything to feed this giant horse. Finally an elderly gentleman appeared who had lived in the States. He took the initiative to help the horse acclimate to the new culture and environment. He also taught the family how to talk to the horse and how to take care of it. Finally things calmed down, the older boys learned how to ride, and the horse learned how to pull the plow through the rocky fields.

It soon was proven that the horse was too much for the family. They could not afford to feed it, they could not afford to make a saddle or samari for it, and the terrain rendered it almost useless. So, the oldest brother decided to take it down to the southern part of Peloponnesus where they had flat land and big valleys and sell the horse. A distant relative paid 800 drachmas for it and sold Thanasis his donkey for 600 drachmas. Thanasis took the 200 remaining drachmas and bought corn. He loaded the donkey with it and returned home. It was the uncle that bought the horse that counseled Thanasis

74

to take the family and move away from the village if they wanted to survive. His advice was, "Bring the family down here, close to Amaliada where you can find food and work. If you stay there while your dad is in jail, all of you will die from hunger or you will get killed." Thanasis objected and said, "We do not have a place where we can live." To which the uncle replied, "Down here you could build a grass hut and live in it. At least you will survive."

Thanasis returned to the village with the donkey, the corn and the newly planted idea of relocation. Little did the family know then that divine providence was leading that way, not only for the survival of the family but also for leading the family into the Gospel light and the redeeming grace of God. Little did they know the move would help to facilitate God's plan for Vasilis' life and the purpose which He had ordained for him.

Thanasis, gently but firmly, broke the news to his mother whose pain and agony could not be put into words. "Mother," he said, "We are going to move south, close to Amaliada. If we stay here we are going to die from hunger or get killed." Her response was emotional and with tears, "My son," she said, "What would we do there with no place to stay, no place to lay our head; strangers without knowing anyone? At least here we have our little house, a few sheep and goats and we are closer to your father who is in jail. We can make it. We will survive. There we would be like strangers without anything." Thanasis was gentle and yet persistent. "Well, mother," he said, "If you want to stay, you can stay. But I will take the children and move south. There is no hope here. We will make it there."

At that moment his mother became very emotional and while crying, the words began to leave her lips, "No, my child. Wherever we go, we go together. Either we live together or we die together!" From that moment forward, things were set into motion for the move, even though no one knew exactly how, where or what would be the outcome. Emotions were like a roller coaster for everyone. One day the song of hope was sung, and the next day it seemed everyone had joined the song of despair. The civil war was intensifying, supplies were getting fewer and fewer, and the clouds of uncertainty were hovering not only over the family, but over the whole country.

In the early part of the summer of 1946, Thanasis devised a plan for the relocation of the family. He would take Christos, his brother and the few sheep and goats the family had and together with an uncle, take them to the town of Damiza in the southern part of Peloponnesus. There he was going to find someone to hire Christos as a shepherd boy with the agreement that he could keep his own flock with him. Then they could locate a temporary place where the family could stay and they could return back and move the whole family.

So, the three of them, Thanasis, Christos and uncle Yianis began the 48 hour journey with a certain number of goats and sheep and two donkeys loaded with supplies. As they started to leave a tearful mother, realizing the dangers on the road and the dangers of the war, she gave the last blessing to her children with these words, "O Theos na sas fotisi kai na sas odigisi paidiamou." – "May God give light in your path and guidance, my children."

There is no accurate information as to how long they traveled and how long Thanasis stayed before he returned to the village. But we do know that a tearful mother never failed day after day to mention their names and ask for God's protection. When she fixed something for supper for the other children as they sat at the table to eat, she would say, "I wonder if my boys have anything to eat."

Thanasis' plan worked out just as he had thought. He found someone who was willing to combine his flock with Christos' flock. This man had both the means and the fields, and Christos was going to be in charge. A cousin of Thanasis' dad offered him a small place next to his house outside of the town which he used it to store hay and keep his horse. He told Thanasis the house could be fixed up and the family could live there. He also encouraged him that they could find work in the fields and that it will be easy for Vasilis and his sister Yeota to go to school. This 16-year-old felt certainty in his heart that the plans were falling into place and divine providence had preceded him and had prepared the way.

When he returned to the village after two or three weeks, Vasilis does not know for sure, it seemed God gave him both insight and wisdom what to do for the safety of the family. He went to the authorities and asked for papers of relocation with signatures and seals, so the family could show to the authorities in other places where they were going to pass through and not be detained. The stage was set for the move. The family probably went to church for the last time in the village, said goodbye to friends and relatives, and Vasilis embraced his only boyhood friend, George Rounis and the only first grade schoolmate that he remembers, Georges Paraskevopoulos. They were ready for the trip. In those days, they did not know anything about refugees or displaced people; they were in search of survival!

It was an early morning in the summer of 1946 that the family loaded all they could on their small donkey and everything each one could carry, locked their modest house, and left the dad behind in jail. With tears in their eyes and apprehension in their heart, they set their sail for the difficult journey that was resting on faith that God would both protect and provide.

Vasilis was both reluctant and resistant to the move but he had no choice and his resistance proved to be a challenge for the rest of the family for the duration of the trip and the first few months in the new place. They had to travel up mountains, down valleys and cross rivers. Their main fear was falling into the hands of antartes (guerrillas). Sometimes they took small breaks for rest and sometimes walked with their shoes in hand because their feet were hurting. They encouraged one another to go on. In the first part of the trip, Vasilis gave them fits. At times he would sit down and not move in spite of his mother's pleas. There were times that he would run backwards pretending that he was going back to the village, but he was scared to do so. At times he would cry and say he wanted water and wanted it now. He tried the patience, and probably the soul, of the whole family.

On the first day of the journey after walking ten or twelve hours and as darkness began to fall, they had arrived in a remote area where there was an old abandoned inn. They settled for the night out of sight behind the inn. It was one of the most fearful nights because both the antartes and the army were traveling at night. Their fear intensified past midnight when they heard, in the small road passing in the front of the inn, the march of either army or antartes. The slightest movement or sound could mean instant death. But the night passed without incident. They had huddled all together against the wall and the presence of some bushes protected them from view.

The second day of the journey began early in the morning. The terrain was friendlier as they began to descend from the mountains to the fertile valleys of Peloponnesus with their orange, lemon and olive groves. Their spirits began to revive; their hopes began to rise that they might make it after all. Vasilis' mother continued to thank God and verbalize her request for protection and guidance.

Vasilis does not recall many details of the journey, as to what they ate, what kind of people they met, except two incidents which are engraved in his mind. He recalls the fear that gripped his heart as they passed the night outside that abandoned inn, not knowing whether they would be alive by morning. He recalls the refreshment they experienced as they came to a water fountain, drank cool water, rested for a while and even threw some water on each other. He recalls that as they descended from the mountains, they began to encounter some fairly good roads. Up to this point they were traveling on what could be perceived as goat paths. It would be difficult to put into words the horror seen on his face when he saw a large object on the road moving toward them in high speed. Not knowing what it was, he ran off the road as far as he could. It was the first time that he saw a motorized vehicle. It was an old, beaten up truck.

There is not much recollection from Vasilis as to where they spent the second night of the journey. But he recalls that they arrived at the house of the relatives located on the hillside overlooking the town of Damiza. It was a two-story stone house occupied by two families surrounded by olive groves and grapevine fields with a water well about 700 or 1000 yards away. Attached to the house was what we call in Greek ahouri, a small building where you store hay and keep the horse in. This was the place that Vasilis and his family were supposed to live. Floors of dirt, horse smell, cobwebs everywhere, one wooden door and no windows. There was no place where you could build a fire. You could imagine what the place looked like. This kind of environment did not help at all with Vasilis' resistance and rebellion to the move, but there were not any choices left.

Soon the family cleaned the place and made beds out of boards and filled mattresses with straw. There were three beds, one for the three boys, one for their sister and one for the mother. There was anticipation that the dad would be released from jail. They fixed the door and made a fireplace for both warmth and cooking. Such confining quarters have their advantages and disadvantages, and they are filled with humorous stories. Even though it is not our aim to get into such stories, one concerning Vasilis will suffice. Since the three boys used only one bed and Vasilis was the youngest, they put him in the middle of the bed so he would not fall off during the night. But Vasilis formed a habit while asleep. He would draw his legs all the way up to his chest and then kick the covers off of the other boys. During the winter that created a problem because it was cold and that displeased his brothers very much. They did not know what to do in order to solve the situation. Finally one of the two older boys came up with the solution. They waited until Vasilis fell asleep, took a rope and tied his legs, and then tied the rope on the bed board. This is what they did. Case closed!

The family settled in the best way they could considering the circumstances and they made the effort to adjust into this new place without a father and under unusual conditions. The mother and the two older boys found jobs and worked in the fields. Vasilis and Yeota started school. From 1946 to 1952, they lived in four different rental houses, two in the country and two in town. In 1952 they built their own house in town. There was little news from the father who was in jail and Vasilis does not recall if the mother was able to make those long trips again and visit him.

Even though the family found relief from one problem, hunger, the other problem, the civil war, now had spread in this area, and it was intensified. Vasilis could share a lot of stories from this period that could make a heart of stone melt. One day the guerrillas would invade the town, the next day the army would come. One day the guerrillas would come in and execute those who they thought had collaborated with the army. The next day the army would come in and execute those who they thought had assisted the guerrillas. There were small battle scrimmages in the area and the sound of the machine gun cannot be forgotten.

Vasilis would never forget the day when the army came into town and arrested certain individuals, including the son of the priest of the town who they thought had ties with the antartes. They loaded the men in an army truck and took them to a place called chavarovrisi, a water fountain surrounded by platanos. The whole town could hear the sound of the machine gun as they were executed. The whole town was covered with a dark blanket of mourning. The most moving moment was one hour later when the army truck pulled from the main road in front of a café and the soldiers began to drop bodies to the ground as if they were bags of potatoes. Young men, middle aged men and old men; laying on the ground with their bellies busted open and their faces all messed up; and their loved ones hovering over them to identify their bodies and take them for proper burial.

Vasilis recalls wiping the tears from his eyes, as a host of feelings of anger mixed with pity were raging within his heart for such an injustice and the infliction of such pain. Seeing people try to console each other for that for which there is no consolation, rips your heart apart and something from within you cries for justice or better said, vengeance. Events like these caused Vasilis to think seriously about life, the nature of man and to reflect on religious matters to which he has been exposed earlier. It was events like these and others in the span of four or five years that altered his thinking, shaped his view of life and began to give focus to his destiny.

He began to dream and fantasize that he was born for something better than and desired to shake off the shackles of poverty and hardship with their untold suffering. Was there a God ordained destination or just the response of misguided human nature? Time would tell!

The cruelty of the civil war continued and the dangers for the family increased. Vasilis' older brother was drafted by the army. The army also took the mule of the neighbor to carry supplies for them from place to place. The family had moved at that time to another house out in the country, about fifteen minutes from town, which was like a mansion in comparison with the others.

One evening the antartes came to town with a disguise and an outpouring of kindness. They gathered in one of the main cafes in town. They had several musical instruments, mbousouki, clarinet, guitars, mandolin and etc. They began to sing, play and dance and give free drinks to everyone. The innocent townspeople gathered around to watch and participate. Soon a big crowd gathered and it gave the appearance of a big party. It appeared everyone had a good time. Vasilis and his two brothers were there. But after a while Vasilis noticed that something rare was taking place. From time to time two guerrillas would take a young man and disappear in the darkness of the night. Vasilis decided to follow from a distance and investigate. To his surprise the young men were taken into the schoolhouse where there were some high-ranking antartes, more guerrillas and a lot of young men. That was a forced draft. They were taking the young men to join the fight whether or not they wanted. When Vasilis saw what was taking place, he ran quickly and advised his brothers and a cousin of his. They quietly slipped out into the darkness in three different directions because the main routes of exit were guarded by the guerrillas. They did not return to the house because the houses quite often were raided.

On another occasion after their father had been released from jail, he and the two older boys were in town early in the evening. They were still living out in the country. The army came in, sealed the town so no one could get out or in. Vasilis' dad and his two brothers were stuck in town for the night. Vasilis, his mother and sister were all alone in the house out in the country sitting at the fireplace. They were not aware that the town had been seized by the army, and as it was getting late they wondered what had happened to the other members of the family and why they were not yet home. They decided to wait around the fireplace, when at midnight an extremely loud knock came at the door. When the door opened, what appeared to be several uniformed guerrillas pushed their way into the house and began to search everything. After they were confident it was safe they came close to the fireplace.

82

Vasilis' mother was very uncomfortable and fearful, and then she took a very bold and dangerous step. She looked at the one who appeared to be the leader and said to him, "If you are antartes (guerrillas), please leave, the army is in town. But if you are the army, sit down and I will fix you something to eat." The man responded to her with a stern and angry voice, "So, that is it? If we are antartes to leave, but if we are the army you will fix us something to eat?" The mother replied boldly, "Yes." At that time he pulled out his gun and said, "I am going to kill you!" At that time Vasilis and his sister Yeota began to cry uncontrollably and hug their mother. It was then he put away his gun and said, "We are the army." But Vasilis' mother refused to believe them. In order to convince her he took off his overcoat to show her his army decorations and uniform, to which she replied, "This does not mean anything. The antartes can wear the same things." At the end it was proven he was army and the rest of the night the house was like a grand station. Soldiers moved in and out all night and having built several bonfires outside, endeavored to warm themselves. That was the tragedy of the civil war; you never knew whether you were talking to a friend or to an enemy.

As the civil war appeared to be coming to an end, the family had moved to town. In 1952 or 1953, they built their new home and began to look for ways to shape their future. Christos was persuaded by his older brother to leave the life of tending the flock and go to school in the island of Leros and become a shoemaker. Yeota was sent to the next town to become a seamstress. Thanasis and his father began to get involved with retail with fruits and vegetables, and later with clothing and other items. Thanasis would go to the city on Saturday and buy wholesale and then on Sunday afternoon or Monday the father would load his donkey and go sell in the villages. That served the family well for a while. Then they bought an irrigated piece of land and they began to farm, planting tomatoes, cucumbers, cabbage, cauliflower, broccoli and other things, for both wholesale and retail.

Vasilis began working while he was yet in school. In the spring he contracted vineyards for cultivation and would work after school. In the summer he worked in a brick factory close to home where everything was made by hand, there was nothing automated. Later he went farther in the cambo and worked with the harvesting machines and even got into the selling business with his brother and dad. By 1952, Thanasis had married to Eleni. He stayed with the family and was the driving force in the business adventures. Christos got back from school, served in the army and sought employment in Athens where later he got involved in the retail business of clothing. It was a time of various changes and events, which prepared the family for some spiritual encounters even though no one was aware of it at the time.

THE AWAKENING OF THE SOUL
AND SPIRITUAL ENCOUNTERS

The town of Damiza

**Vasilis in the vineyard with
the grapes.**

"Now when they heard this, they were pricked in their heart, and said to Peter and to the apostles, Men and brethren, what shall we do? Then Peter said unto them, Repent, and be baptized every one of you in the name of Jesus Christ for the remission of sins, and ye shall receive the gift of the Holy Ghost"
Acts 2:37-38.

Vasilis finished the sixth grade in the top of his class. Due to the fact that high schools existed only in the big cities, the conditions of the family and some other circumstances, it was not feasible for him at that time to continue his education; or could it be that divine providence had a purpose for that delay? He had a keen interest in learning, great thirst for knowledge, and he had begun to experience dissatisfaction with things the way they were. Even though he was young he began to experience some kind of religious or spiritual awakening. He began to feel bad and he was condemned for a lot of the things he was doing as a child. He began to have thoughts about God and about death and he was afraid.

One day he was caught in a storm out in the country. Suddenly the sky turned dark and there was lightning and thunder, and rain and hail began to fall furiously. He was so afraid that he thought he was going to die. As he was running for his life, he began to pray to God and Virgin Mary. He promised if they could get him out of the storm alive, he would do anything. He would light candles in their honor or anything. It was fifteen or twenty minutes later that he found refuge in a country home. He was shocked and crying till the storm passed by. Afterward, he began to attend the Greek Orthodox Church somewhat regularly and even began to help the priest a few times as an altar boy. He was somewhat intrigued by the liturgy of the church, monasticism and the priesthood. In fact they occupied his mind quite often.

There were two specific encounters which were going to intensify his spiritual awakening. One of those encounters was a priest of the churches who came from the city to this small town each Thursday evening and give a homily to the people that gathered to hear him. His talk was centered on the Gospels. Vasilis had several conversations with him and having seen Vasilis' interest and thirst for knowledge; he recommended that Vasilis read the Bible.

The second encounter was with a fellow named Nikos Grybas. Nikos had just returned to town from prison. He had deserted the army and when he was captured he was jailed and awaiting trial. While in jail someone gave him a New Testament and in the process of reading it and receiving some counsel, he turned his life over to the Lord, repented, asked for forgiveness. As a result, his life was genuinely changed. When time came for his trial, he stood before the court and took full responsibility for his actions, apologized and shared with them how God had changed his life through reading the New Testament and promised that he was going to be a good citizen. He said he would accept the court's decision, no matter what. To his surprise and the surprise of everyone else he was acquitted. While in prison he had learned a trait of art, working with gypsum and painting. It was his work that interested Vasilis. He wanted to learn how to do it and he tried for a while. It was the engagement in these two encounters that guided his search for spiritual matters.

Vasilis was not aware at the time that his brother Thanasis was in a soul-searching journey. He always had religious tendencies, and he was a singer in the Greek Orthodox Church, but all in the nominal level. He too had approached Nikos Grybas, not so much for his spiritual knowledge, but because he wanted to learn the trait of his art. But there was not much conversation, if any, between Vasilis and Thanasis on spiritual things, even though Thanasis was protective of his little brother.

Vasilis' dissatisfaction with life and his thirst for knowledge continued and he was almost ready to grasp anything that promised some help. It was during this time that he was brought face to face with a New Testament. He has no recollection whatsoever from where or how this New Testament reached him; only speculations, no certainties. (About a year ago Vasilis was told by his brother Thanasis that it was he who had given Vasilis the New Testament. It was brought by his brother Christos when he returned from the island Leros where he had gone to learn a trade.)

Vasilis approached the New Testament the same way that a thirsty boy who was dying of thirst would approach a fountain of crystal clear water. He read it daily. He spent hours a week with nothing else but the New Testament. He underlined and memorized it. Quite often he spent hours at night with the aid of a kerosene lamp reading. The more he read, the more his soul was awakened and the more intense the desire and the search became. Being influenced by the Greek Orthodox Church and having knowledge of the monastic life whose aim it was to find redemption and freedom from temptation as well as purity of the soul, he engaged in prolonged fasting from meat and etc. He chastised his body with disciplines and actions which are not permissible to share. He would wake up at night to read and make formal prayers that he knew. Through all these the Holy Spirit at the same time was working in his life in guidance, assistance and revelation concerning the truth.

Although he did not know what to call it at that time, the Word began to grip Vasilis' heart and it was evident the Holy Spirit had brought conviction. There were several times that he prayed for forgiveness in the same fashion. But one day in particular, and some details escape Vasilis here, as he was sitting on the side of the hill reading his New Testament, the account where Jesus was questioned by Pilate. Pilate asked the multitudes, "What must I do with Jesus?" It seemed that the Spirit of God moved upon Vasilis and the question had become a personal one, "What would you do with Jesus?" It was at that moment Vasilis was overtaken with emotion, began to cry and ask God for forgiveness. In the meantime the Holy Spirit was revealing that salvation was through the shed blood of Christ on the cross and by faith in Jesus Christ. There was a measure of thankfulness and joyfulness that filled his heart and there was the emergence of a confidence that God had forgiven him which changed both his attitude and outlook. He felt at that time he was the only one that had such an experience with the Lord.

Vasilis did not know a lot of details of what was going on in the life of his older brother Thanasis. Though there were several superficial discussions about spiritual things, there was not much intimate information shared. But Thanasis at the same time was in a spiritual journey and search of his own. He, too, had conversations with the young man Nikos Grybas and at some point had made a commitment to the Lord. It seemed that suddenly a lot of things came into the open. Nikos and his sister Niki, Thanasis and his wife Eleni, Vasilis and his sister Yeota, began to meet together to study the Bible. First they met at Nikos' house, but when there were some objections by his father, they met at Vasilis' house. There were a few times they studied the Word and had prayer in the moonlight.

The faith of Vasilis began to be intensified and he was grasping for anything that would help him grow in the Lord. He developed a very consistent prayer life even though he was not that familiar with the mechanics of prayer. He endeavored to be obedient to the word and had made some efforts for witnessing in his own way. He does not recall all the circumstances and the events that led into it, but he decided to follow the Lord in baptism. He recalls that it was out in the country in a water pond and that the weather was very cold. He recalls there were about five people present, but could not recall either faces or names. He recalls that he was baptized by Nikos Grybas, but he could not recall who else was baptized with him, except that they almost froze to death as they tried to get back to town all wet. It was about two years ago where Vasilis engaged his older brother in serious conversation that the memory of Vasilis was refreshed. When Vasilis' brother saw him getting baptized, he came under conviction that he should follow the Lord in baptism also and he was baptized.

So Vasilis and his oldest brother, Thanasis, were baptized together.

There were two things that took place during the time. Some members of the family could not understand why the group who claimed to be so religious would not attend church services in the Greek Orthodox Church. The talk among the townspeople was that they were heretics and against the Greek Orthodox Church. In the most cases the townspeople tried to keep their distance from them. On the other hand in a small town called Tragano, there was a small Free Evangelical Church which was pastored by a graceful, white-haired, white-bearded gentleman named Elias Paraskevopoulos. In that congregation was a lay evangelist, Thanasis Lygopoulos, who was both charismatic and aggressive. He was from a group of people in that town called gypsies, but they were not gypsies as such. A great number of them dedicated themselves in the weaving of baskets. Some historians say that they had emigrated from Egypt many, many years ago.

They had heard about Vasilis and the group in the small town of Damiza; about those who had left the Greek Orthodox Church and they called them heretics. This lay evangelist decided to make the hour-and-a-half trip by bus and explore the situation. When he arrived the group met together, and being an evangelist, he began to expound the Word evangelistically, centering on the death and resurrection of Christ and in the need for repentance and faith. Being aggressive he asked Vasilis two questions, "By what means does one get salvation?" Vasilis' response was, "Through the shed blood of Christ on the cross." "How does one obtain salvation?" was his second question. And the response was, "By faith in Jesus Christ and his death on the cross." He responded to Vasilis, "Then, you are born again." It was the first time that Vasilis had heard those words, and he had no idea of their meaning. Vasilis developed a close relationship with him that lasted for years, and had a great impact on his life and his spiritual formation.

As Vasilis was falling in love with the Lord and His word, it was summer time and he was working in a brick factory. Since their house was a big open space without rooms, he got the bright idea that he was going to use the money he earned to build a small room in one of the corners of the house for privacy and meditation. He was sixteen at that time. He has no recollection of who assisted him in building the room but with its dimensions 8 x 7 or 10 x 10, it was finished soon and it became Vasilis' refuge. It was his sanctuary. He wrote verses of scripture on each wall and even on the ceiling and soon the room became the meeting place for the small group.

Pastor Elias Paraskevopoulos with family.

On Christmas Eve in 1954 or 1955 the group spent most of the evening in that room in scripture reading, prayer and conversation. By Christmas morning they had decided they were going to visit the little church in Tragano. They never had been in a church like this before. The journey was long and difficult by foot. They spent most of the day walking in the rain through difficult terrain, crossing rivers and going over hills. That night the church had a service and a good number of young people were present. It was the first time that the group heard hymns being sung, prayers offered and the word preached. Vasilis testifies that he probably spent most of the time crying and he recalls that the elderly pastor, Elias, approached him and said, "Vasilis, the Lord does not want us to cry, He wants us to rejoice." It was that night that Vasilis developed a lasting friendship with the two young men from that congregation, Takis and Nikos.

Takis Manetas

As Vasilis progressed in his walk with the Lord he became a fervent young evangelist. He visited people in other villages and shared the word in his simple way. In fact, he was influential in one village by introducing a young man and his family to the truth of the gospel, who later became his sister's husband. His witness resulted in many confrontations with both priests and police. At one time a policeman told Vasilis if he were to hear him again witnessing about Christ, he was going to hang him from a tree with his head down. There were occasions, since the town priest was not very educated, that they would bring

Vasilis with Nikos

an educated priest from the city to gather the people in the main square of the town and talk about the heretics, evangelists or protestants. Vasilis would attend these meetings quite often, lean on the corner of one of the buildings and listen. In the meantime he was gathering ammunition for defense.

On a particular night, the visiting priest had gathered the people in the town square and he had begun his attack on Vasilis and the group in a rather animated way. He was loud and appeared to have been angry. Vasilis had taken his regular place, leaning against the wall with shorts on and with a reserved or rather bashful disposition. The Priest was admonishing the people not to have anything to do with them because they were the enemies of the church. The mayor interrupted him and said, "We have one of them here tonight" and pointed to Vasilis, motioning him at the same time to come where the priest was standing. The priest began to bombard Vasilis with difficult questions, and Vasilis would answer with a verse of scripture saying, "What about this?" The priest had no answer to explain that which the scripture states. After several of such scriptures without a straight answer from the priest, it was noticed by all that the priest was getting agitated and the crowd was divided in two. Some of them began to say, "Don't you see? He is a priest, educated and a teacher and he cannot answer the questions of a young man." When Vasilis saw the division in the crowd and that a great number began to support him, he became bolder, the priest became angrier and he walked away, which exonerated Vasilis in the eyes of the people.

TRANSFORMING ENCOUNTERS

Vasilis sensed some dissatisfaction and restlessness within himself. He did not have a justifiable reason for the feelings. It seemed there was discouragement due to the prevailing negative attitude with his surroundings. One evening he decided to go a short distance from the house into an olive grove and spend some time in prayer and meditation. It was a renewing experience with a sense of the presence of God, warmth of His love, a feeling of overflowing peace, joy and contentment. After a while a fear gripped his heart and a sense of uncertainty that forced him to ask the question, "Lord, what do I do now?" While he was walking back toward the house the thought came to his mind, "Vasilis, why don't you spend some time in fasting and prayer and you will see the glory of God!" So, he made an unorthodox resolution, that he would lock himself in the little room that he had made and he would spend time in fasting and prayer till he heard from God.

There were different reactions to his decision by the family. His mother thought that he was going to die. His sister challenged him that she had seen other Christians who did not behave that way. One evening his mother expressed some concern to his father about Vasilis and his father in a joking way responded, "If he wants to die, let him die." Vasilis was intense in his prayer and he was seeking direction. If his memory does not deceive him, he spent four days and five nights in the room. In the last evening he was reading the story of Hezekiah, whom God had advised through the prophet Isaiah to set his house in order because he was going to die. Upon hearing the words of the Lord, Hezekiah turned his face toward the wall and prayed, "Now, Lord, remember that I have walked before you with a perfect heart and I have done that which is right in your sight." The Lord spared his life for 15 years. The story had an impact on Vasilis. He was convinced that everything was going to be okay. He broke his fast and began to engage in life.

Sometime later there was a young people's meeting in the city of Patra, about 2 or 2½ hours by bus from his place. Some of the group was able to go, but Vasilis, due to lack of money and some other factors, did not go. He wanted to go and he was very disappointed. It was late in the afternoon while grazing his horse on the side of the road, that a lady friend of the family passed by and asked Vasilis why he had not gone with the rest of the group. Vasilis gave his reason to which she responded, "I think you should go and I will pay your bus ticket." Vasilis made quick arrangements with his mom and dad. He arrived in the room where his friends Takis, Costas, and Nikos were staying, before the evening service started. His friends tried to make Vasilis presentable for the evening service. They tried to put a tie on him, but he refused. They tried to fix his hair and take away that country look from him, but to no avail. He does not remember a lot about the trip or the service except the surprise on the face of the others to see him there.

One of the things that made such a great impact on Vasilis was on the second day in the afternoon where he found himself with two older young people in the house of the pastor, Menelaus Katsarkas. He was a Spirit-filled, gray-haired, charismatic older gentleman with a glow of heaven on his face and whose lips dripped with the honey of constant praise and truth. The three of them found themselves in his living room where he began to expound the truth about the fullness of the Spirit and the life of holiness. His attention was given primarily to the older youth, but Vasilis was very attentive and in his heart was repeating the words, 'This is what I need. This will deliver me from my struggles with temptation."

In the process of the conversation he came to a closing point and asked both young men if they would be willing to surrender to the Lord and receive the fullness of the Spirit. It was apparent that both of them were resisting. He tried again the second time with a very gentle and compassionate spirit and their resistance became evident. Then without any signs of warning turned to Vasilis and said, "Vasilis, what about you?" "Yes," responded Vasilis, "I want to pray that God will fill me with His Spirit." It was an eventful and joyful time as he laid hands on Vasilis and both prayed for the fullness of the Spirit. As Vasilis recounts the event there is certain emotion that comes through. He recalls there was no doubt the Holy Spirit descended upon him. He testifies of peace, joy, victory and confidence filling his heart and the change that came upon his life and his demeanor was noticed by all.

The third thing that Vasilis remembers of that meeting which had a lasting impact upon his life, in fact it altered the outlook of his ministry later; was during the third day when some of the young people suggested they should go to visit sister Katerina Tsonopoulou. She was an elderly sister who was ill and living in a small room on the top of a flat roof in one of the houses. Vasilis had no idea that sister Katerina was a fervent evangelist who with her bold witness for the Lord had made a name for herself throughout the state of Elias. There were so many bold stories about her witnessing that it was hard to believe them. It had been told that one time in a heated confrontation with the Bishop of the Greek Orthodox Church, that she called him a donkey due to his lack of understanding of spiritual things. But many testify everywhere that they had come to the Lord because of her witness and faithfulness.

Vasilis was totally unprepared for what he saw and experienced that day. As they climbed the winding metal stairs to the top of the roof and entered the small room, there was a small, frail, elderly lady in her 80s, her body covered with sores but her spirit was soaring with the angels and a heavenly glow was set on her face. She had no family except the family of God that looked after her.

As the young people gathered around her and began to sing a few choruses, it appeared that the Spirit of God came upon her. She was revitalized and with the fervency of the evangelist that she was, she began to expound the word of God and to exhort the young people to remain obedient and faithful to the Lord. As they were coming to the conclusion of the visit, sister Katerina looked toward Vasilis and motioned to him to come close to her. Then she looked upon him and said, "I want to pray for you and I want to bless you." She placed her feeble hands on Vasilis' head and before she prayed and gave him her blessing, she quoted the following scripture, "Those who sow in tears shall reap in joy. He who continually goes forth weeping, bearing seed for sowing, shall doubtless come again with rejoicing, bringing his sheaves with him" (Psalm 126:5-6). Then she began to pray with all the urgency and the passion of heaven that the content of the scripture would be Vasilis' passion and ministry. "It would be difficult to put into words the feeling, the atmosphere and the sacredness of the moment," says Vasilis. "In that moment I felt that I was commissioned, ordained and sent forth with both authority and unction that never left me to this day." He states, "This took place in 1956, and even today when I think about it, chills run down my spine and I want to reexamine it, ask for God's forgiveness and for a rekindling of the passion and the urgency."

There was another memorable encounter for Vasilis that helped set him aflame with the spirit of evangelism. After a few days back in his town, he felt impressed to catch the bus and go to a couple villages where there were some people known for witnessing. But to his surprise all three buses going to those villages that day were completely full. No one was taken from the town. The Bible says that "God works in all things together for good to those who love him." That was the case with Vasilis, as soon as he returned home, he had an acute appendix attack, and he was rushed into the city hospital where he had an emergency surgery. If he had gone to the villages, we do not know if he would have survived.

The day after the surgery, while still in the hospital, he received some notable visitors who were going to play a significant role in God's plan for his life. They were Nick and Rose Zazanis, missionaries with the Church of God in Athens and also a young man with them named Nicholas. They had heard about Vasilis and they had gone to his town to visit him. When

Vasilis with Nick Zazanis

they found that he was in the hospital, they made the extra thirty minutes trip to Amaliada to see him. The Zazanises had a great love for young people, especially for those whose lives has been touched by the Master and who had expressed interest in ministry. After the introductions Vasilis did not lose the opportunity to share his testimony and expressed his willingness to serve the Lord wherever He wanted him. The Zazanises concluded the visit with prayer and committed each other to the grace of God and the promise that they were going to keep in touch.

The day Vasilis was released from the hospital, his friends from Tragano, Takis, Costas, Nikos and some other people had come to see him. They decided to spend the evening with the pastor and the small congregation in Amaliada. The next day they were going to catch the train and spend a couple days in Tragano before Vasilis returned to his town. They always used the train trips as an opportunity to distribute Christian tracts and evangelize. Normally Takis was the main spokesman. Five minutes before the stop for the exit, all of them would stand up in the middle of the car of the train, Takis would share a brief word from the Word and then they would go the opposite direction distributing tracts and then would go out from the exit.

It was two weeks later that Vasilis received a letter from Athens. It was from Brother Zazanis. He had written to Vasilis to express how pleased he was to meet him and informed him it appeared the Lord might be opening a door for Vasilis to travel to Athens. He informed him that he thought there was a job opening and that he could have a ministry in the church with the young people, help with the visitation and with the publication of the Gospel Trumpet (Salpiga Tou Evanggeliou) in Greek. It is not clear how and when Vasilis responded to that letter, but he spent considerable time in prayer, seeking direction from the Lord. In fact, he had asked for some signs if that was God's will for him and then waited on the Lord as we are admonished in the scripture.

THE JOURNEY TO ATHENS

When the time came and it was made clear that Vasilis should accept the invitation of Brother Zazanis, Vasilis decided he should go, providing the Lord made provision for the transportation and some other expenses. He talked with his parents. Without any hesitation his Dad made provision for the expenses. So armed with faith and the certainty that this was God's will for his life he set his sail toward Athens. At that time he had no knowledge of the impact the trip would have in his life and of the journey that God was preparing for him. The full support of the family, and the promise that God would be with him as he was about to walk into this newly opened door, was encouraging.

Vasilis does not recall all the details that transpired after arriving in Athens. He was not fully prepared and he did not anticipate the challenges, crises, some conflicts and the temptations which were going to welcome him to Athens. Always there were that providential angel placed by God to help him remain within God's will and serve as supportive pillars in his journey of faith. Vasilis became aware more than ever that "The angel of the Lord encampeth around about those who fear Him"(Ps. 34:7 KJV), and circumstances forced him to find refuge in some of the old hymns and quite often sang them with deep emotion, "When the storms of life around me beating, when rough the path that I have trod, within my closet door retreating, I love to be alone with God." "Alone with God, the world forbidden, alone with God, O blest retreat! Alone with God, and in him hidden, to hold with him, communion sweet."[1] Another song which captivated his soul and echoed in the depths of his heart daily was, "His Eye Is On the Sparrow", especially the phrase, "I know He watches over me." [2] There are times we are forced by circumstances to cast our anchor in the promises of God and hold on to His unchanging faithfulness.

The journey to Athens at that time was between five and six hours by train. Vasilis arrived in the late afternoon at 17 Zaimi Street where the church was located, and the residence of Brother Zazanis. The Zazanises introduced Vasilis to Stylianos and Stella Charalambakis, who were serving as the associates of Brother Zazanis. Stylianos was a highly educated priest in the Greek Orthodox Church whom Brother Zazanis had won to the Lord. Later, with a gentle spirit, using their own writings and in the light of the New Testament, he wrote about a dozen books on theology and exposing the errors of the Greek Orthodox Church.

Vasilis with the Zazanises and the Charalambakises

Vasilis stayed in the guest room of the church. The next day Brother Zazanis took him to see the man who had promised him a job. The visit went quite well in the beginning and Vasilis shared freely his testimony. When finally Brother Zazanis asked the gentleman about the job that he had promised for Vasilis, he looked at Vasilis and said, "Young man, I think that you will make a good preacher, but I do not have a job for you!" Both Zazanis and Vasilis were disappointed, not knowing what could be the next step. But in spite of it all, God still was working out His purpose.

Sometime later, (or it could have been the following Sunday), Brother Zazanis asked Vasilis to share his testimony with the church and the young people. The response was both enthusiastic and positive. As a result Brother Zazanis invited him to stay in the guest room and shared with him that probably the Lord had brought him to Athens to minister in the church, with the young people, the visitation, and help with the publishing of the Gospel Trumpet. Zazanis was a charismatic, enthusiastic, zealous leader who always radiated love. He was strong with the pen and in visitation. His preaching was exhortative and biblical. He had an unconditional love for young people and he trusted them to a fault. His passion was to see young men enter the ministry and he encouraged them with anything possible. He always took Vasilis with him in visitation, allowed him to share freely in the discussion and always asked him to lead in prayer. He began to give him some responsibilities in the church office and some assignments for specific ministry.

Soon Vasilis developed strong relationships with all age groups in the congregation and quite often was called upon to minister to their needs. He was given the opportunity to visit other people outside Athens in small towns who had expressed their interest in the Gospel truth and the church. On one occasion he was sent to visit a family outside the city of Patra to encourage them in the Lord because there was no church there. That night as their guest, as he was sharing the word around the fireplace, he led their two boys to accept Christ as their savior. In another occasion, when a congregation of the Church of God had started in Tragano, Vasilis was sent there for several weeks to minister. He put together the drama of the prodigal son as an evangelism tool and it was viewed by hundreds of people with good results.

Since God knew what was ahead for Vasilis, his needs and the circumstances that he was going to encounter, He had raised up a small network of individuals whom Vasilis calls providential angels. In fact throughout the story Vasilis claims that in every station of his journey of faith, God has placed those individuals who always proved to be invaluable.

Two of those providential angels were and elderly couple named Jim and Margarita Athanasiadis. When they were very young they had immigrated to the United States and now they had retired and returned to Greece. Since they did not have any children, they gave their time and everything in the ministry of the church. They had a gentle, sweet and hospitable spirit. They loved young people and made every effort to encourage them and be helpful to those who were called to God's work.

Jim and Margarita Athanasiadis on the right with people in the front of the church

They took Vasilis under their wings. They loved him, guided him, prayed for him and quite often had him in their lovely home for delicious home cooked meals. The impact they had on Vasilis' life and spiritual development cannot be put into words. Vasilis recalls that on a particular Sunday, after the service, Brother Jim told Vasilis to clear his day on the following Thursday from 9:00 a.m. to 2:00 p.m.; he was going to come to pick him up and they had some things to do. By nine o'clock he was at the church, and the first place he took Vasilis was to a newly opened clothing store that specialized in ready-made suits. (At that time in Greece, a ready-made suit was not a common thing. Most of the suits were tailor made.) He looked at Vasilis and said to him, 'I want you to select a suit. I am going to buy it for you." Vasilis was both embarrassed and proud and resisted strongly. Probably we should say he resisted stubbornly. Brother Jim took him on the side and in a gentle and loving way counseled him with these words, "Vasilis, God has called you. You are God's man and He wants His men to look nice. God has placed us here to help you fulfill God's call for your life. Don't be proud and resist what God wants to do in your life through His people." Such a spirit and such words completely disarmed Vasilis and he was left without any defense. He recalls that he bought a striped, light gray suit with shirt and tie which he enjoyed for a long time.

After the clothing store, he took Vasilis to a nice restaurant where they enjoyed a nice meal and warm fellowship. Gestures like this one both confirmed and affirmed Vasilis in his pursuing God's will. Brother Jim was indeed God's providential angel in human form that had a significant impact.

During that period in Vasilis' life there were the following people who played a significant role in his spiritual formation and in pursuing the plan of God for the future. Brother Nick Zazanis and his wife Rose with their spirit of love, hospitality and spirit of encouragement combined with the opportunity for service contributed greatly for Vasilis' establishment in the truth and to get a feeling for ministry in the church. The best learning in life does not come from school or books, even though both of them are essential. The best learning comes from observing people and being taught by them, and the Zazanises with their example provided that teaching tool.

Then there was pastor Menelaus Katsarkas who had introduced Vasilis to the life of the Holy Spirit and the life of holiness in Patra. At that time he had accepted a small church in one of the suburbs of Athens, laboring with missionaries Pappas and Diavastis, missionaries with the Oriental Missionary Society from the U.S.A. Menelaus continued to serve as Vasilis' mentor in the deeper life. He always provided helpful books, scriptural truth which we tend to overlook and warm fellowship and hospitality with the constant spirit of encouragement and the example of holy living. They were operating a small Bible Institute that drew Vasilis that direction for warm theological discussion. His good friend Takis was a student there. Takis was one of those young people Vasilis greatly admired and he was inspired by his love for the Lord and his commitment to His will. There was another friend from Tragano that had come to Athens for work, Nikos. He and Vasilis roomed together for about a year.

All these relationship provided both support and encouragement for Vasilis as well as direction in fulfilling God's future plans for ministry. He was so intense and so thirsty for knowledge and spiritual growth. He sought the assistance of a capable young man to tutor him "in" the grammar of ancient Greek. He also accepted the offer from a bright, radiant eighty-year-old Seventh Day Adventist lady to teach him English. She had the sweetest and most loving spirit toward young people, especially those who were on a spiritual journey or quest. She was more interested in teaching Vasilis theology than she was teaching him English.   Nevertheless, Vasilis got a dose of both of them.

At that time Vasilis was in a holding period, because he was waiting for his turn to be drafted in the Greek Army. Every young man upon turning 21 years old has to serve for two years. It was during that waiting period that Zazanis left for a six-month furlough to the U.S.A. and in 1958 a young couple from the United States came to tend the church together with the Charalambakises, Dan and Allita Dallas.   Dan was handsome with black curly hair with an athletic build, positive attitude, friendly and full of enthusiasm. Allita was tall, blond, and blue-eyed and had the most sweet and gentle spirit. She had all the characteristics of a genuine lady, and even though she was somewhat shy, she had the ideal disposition of a pastor's wife. Dan was the son of a Greek immigrant from the Chicago area and Allita was part of what was known then as the Loppen Sisters in the Church of God, a trio that sang on the Christian Brotherhood Hour and at the Anderson Camp Meeting.   Dan had some working knowledge of the Greek language. Allita also had some knowledge of the Greek language. Both of them with eagerness, discipline and commitment worked hard to integrate with the people and did so very effectively.

Their arrival to the church in Athens served as a breath of fresh air. They engaged the young people and instituted wholesome activities both for the church in Athens and the church in Tragano. They were about 25 or 30 years ahead of their time. The youth began to thrive and

Dan and Allita Dallas

that was a very good time for Vasilis. He learned a great deal from his working with the Dallases, he was exposed to different thought and approaches and began to understand himself better. Both of them were genuine and not pretentious.

During that time two other people played a significant role. There was a group of tourists from the United States that visited the church in the summer and they asked Vasilis to accompany them to their visit to Acropolis and Mar's Hill. Among them was a retired public school teacher named Nilah Basham, from Oak Hill, West Virginia. She took some pictures of Vasilis and upon returning to the States she sent some

Vasilis with Dan Dallas

copies to him. Wanting to thank her, he decided to write a letter and say, "Thank you for the pictures. I liked them very much." Instead, he wrote in his broken English, "The pictures liked me very much, thank you!" Nilah never let him live this down.

The other person was an elderly sister of Greek descent from Chicago, who had visited the church with her daughter, Agnes. She maintained consistent correspondence with Vasilis, especially since her daughter married Dinos, the young man who was tutoring Vasilis in the Greek Grammar. It was later when Vasilis faced some challenging times and was about to return back to his hometown, that she wrote him a letter responsible for changing his mind. In fact that letter brought one of the most significant turning points in his life. It is for that reason Vasilis speaks so often about those providential angels placed in his journey by God. Words spoken in the name of Christ, letters written in the name of Christ and acts of love expressed in His name can serve as doors to lead people into God's will and direct them to His purpose.

Although it was filled with a lot of challenges, and with some undesirable experiences, the last year in Athens was filled with many rewarding experiences. Then he was ready to leave for the army. The Holy Spirit was working in his life, his relationship with the Dallases and the Zazanises was very rewarding and he developed some strong disciplines with the Word and prayer. He began to claim the promises from the word, "Call unto me and I will answer thee, and shew thee and mighty things, which thou knowest not" (Jer. 33:3 KJV). He was determined to trust God fully and another promise from the word that he began to claim was from the prophet Hosea, "And My people, shall never be ashamed."(Joel 2:27 KJV).

Also he had resolved in his heart that no matter what the obstacles, what the setbacks, or whatever failure, he would never stay down, he would always get up and take the next step toward the goal. If the spirit of discouragement seemed to knock at his door or the clouds of despair began to rise on the horizon, he would always say to himself, "I can do all things through Christ who strengthens me" (Phil. 4:13 NKJV), and with the reliance of faith, "My God shall supply all your needs" (Phil. 4:19 NKJV). If Michael Ervin was living in his time and had used the words that made him well known in some circles, probably Vasilis would have quoted them quite often, *Look up, Stand up, Never give up.*

1. Johnson Oatman, Jr., *Alone with God, Worship the Lord, Hymnal of the church of God,* Warner Press, Anderson, Indiana, 1989, No. 337.

2. Civilla D. Martin, *His Eyes Is on the Sparrow, Worship the Lord, Hymnal of the Church of God,* Warner Press, Anderson, Indiana, 1989, No. 648.

THE JOURNEY IN THE GREEK ARMY, DISCIPLINE AND DIRECTION

Vasilis

Christos   **Vasilis**   **Thanasis**

"Thou therefore endure hardness, as a good soldier of Jesus Christ. No man that warreth entangleth himself with the affairs of this life; that he may please him who hath chosen him to be a soldier"

II Timothy 2:3-4.

There were several areas in Vasilis' life where he was shy and reserved. Yet, there were other areas where he was confident. When his time was approaching to report in the army base, his brother Christos who had served for two years was trying to give him some advice how to respond during the basic training and how to watch for certain pitfalls. He advised him of the kind of treatment he was going to receive and that he would not have the freedom to do as he pleased. Vasilis responded rather boastfully that there were certain things that would not happen to him in the army and certain things that he would not do. Christos responded to his boastful expression, "Okay, little brother!" Vasilis fired right back, "Okay, what?" Very calmly but firmly Christos responded, "There is one thing that you will learn when you get in the Greek Army." "And what is that?" asked Vasilis. "You will find out that where reason stops, the Greek Army begins," was Christos' response. These words never escaped Vasilis the 24 months that he spent in the service. Time after time during basic training where efforts were made to indoctrinate the new recruits on the glory of Greece and that it has given enlightenment to other nations around the world, Vasilis remembered the words of his brother.

When Vasilis received his notice to report to the Cavalry branch of the army in Kalamata, which was operating with real horses and mules, he was somewhat surprised. He left Athens and went home to spend a few days with the family and thus prepare for his trip. The day before he left for the base, he decided he was going to take with him his Bible, Martin Luther's biography and a small Greek-English dictionary, even though he was told they would not allow him to keep anything. The next day he and his sister Yeota boarded the bus for the two hours or so trip to Kalamata. He was determined that he was not going to report in till the last minute because he did not want his head to be shaved. He reported in about 6:00 p.m. and since everything was closing at that time he achieved his objectives.

In the first days of basic training, Vasilis could not understand how anyone would want to make a career of the military. He did not object so much to the physical exercise and the discipline of the constant marches and the inspections, but he disliked the food and the indoctrination which was intended to break down individualism and make you a property of the state in thinking. What surprised him most was that none of his superiors objected to his books. When he read his Bible or bowed his head for prayer some of his fellow soldiers would make fun of him, and some were wondering why he had the freedom to have books, but none dared to ask.

Halfway into the basic training, on a Thursday morning, some of the mysteries began to unfold. He did not know he was being watched due to the fact that his papers stated that he was Protestant and not Greek Orthodox, like everyone else. That had raised a suspicion because of the tensions with Communism at that time, the aggressive opposition of the Greek Orthodox Church to the Protestant and the refusal of the Jehovah Witness to bear arms and submit to the state. These three were considered to be enemies of the state.

Early that morning he volunteered to give blood and then prepare for the inspection of a high-ranking official who was going to visit the base. The whole thing was over by noon and after lunch Vasilis returned to his quarters. He was not there long when he had the surprise of his life; the army police showed up and called his name. Once Vasilis was identified, they informed him that the head of the base, the major, wanted to see him in his office. That is not a common thing in the Greek Army and Vasilis was wondering about the meaning of all this. On the way to the office he began to fantasize. He thought it could be that his relative who was working in the Army Headquarters in Athens was pulling some strings to keep him in Athens after the basic training so he could go to school at night. But nothing was for certain.

When Vasilis entered the base office and gave the proper salute and stood at attention, the major got up from behind his desk, addressed Vasilis as Mr., using his last name and then shook hands with him. That surprised Vasilis because it was not the proper treatment of a soldier (expressing gentleness and respect), and he was wondering what was going on. The major thanked Vasilis for coming and then turned around and introduced Vasilis to a priest who was standing close on the back side of the open door. Vasilis recognized the name. He was professor of Theology in the University of Athens, and he had written a book against evangelicals in Greece. Vasilis had read the book. The major looked at Vasilis and the professor priest and said, "I want you two to spend the afternoon together."

So Vasilis and the professor began their stroll throughout the base. Sometimes they would lean on a fence, other times they would sit on a bench, and quite often they would stand in the middle of the street, their eyes interlocked with each other, hands waving in the air, engaging in heated theological discussions. Vasilis did not know it, but the priest professor was brought from Athens to the base with the purpose of converting Vasilis back to the Greek Orthodox Church. What a task! It appeared that Vasilis did not have a chance with this learned man of the cloth, but his heart was fired up since he was reading the biography of Martin Luther and he was so entrenched in the Word of God and the wisdom of the Holy Spirit. The conversation took many facets and the professor would always quote from the traditions of the church in order to convince Vasilis that he was in error. But Vasilis would always quote a verse of scripture and then say, "What about this scripture? Should we not obey it?" This conversation continued for hours and appeared that neither one had convinced the other; with the exception that the professor began to get somewhat irritated because he did not know how to deal with the scriptures Vasilis was quoting. Finally after four hours while both of them were leaning against the fence, the priest threw both hands up in the air and looking at Vasilis shouted, "You are beyond help", and he walked away.

Vasilis walked back to his quarters wondering of the effect that this encounter was going to have, not knowing what kind of report the priest was going to give to the major and what kind of recommendations. But Vasilis was convinced that he should always rely on the scriptures and he was happy for having the opportunity to testify of the saving grace of Jesus Christ; the rest was left in the hands of God.

Even though Vasilis had no idea of the outcome concerning his encounter with the priest, one thing became very clear; everyone knew he had been invited to the major's office. They thought he had some special influence, and they began to react differently around him and throw some pointers during their conversation concerning his special treatment.

After Vasilis finished his basic training in Southern Greece he was transferred to a base on the Northern part of Greece close to the borders of Albania, Yugoslavia and Bulgaria, close to the lake Doirani, the place where both the Italians and the Germans crossed into Greece during the war. He spent 21 months in that place, receiving training in most of the weapons, riding with the Cavalry, purchasing agent for his company, secretary in keeping account of the supplies and distributing agent of food to the guards at the borders.

While Vasilis was settling in his new location and with his new responsibilities, there were several new developments that took place. Although Vasilis had not pursued formal education in college, in fact he had not even finished high school at that time, everyone, including his superiors, perceived Vasilis to be a university student. Quite often they removed him from the line to go and work in the office. Such treatment soon spread the rumor that Vasilis was working with the secret service of the army. Of course, this was totally unfounded.

Second, Vasilis had developed correspondence with a young person from a church youth group in the state of Iowa. In one of the letters was enclosed a copy of the youth magazine, REACH, from the Church of God, which would later to play a major role in Vasilis' life.

Third, Vasilis took a three or four-day pass and he went to Athens. While in Athens he decided to visit the Army headquarters where a distant relative was working. His relative held the rank of general. In fact, he had the same last name as Vasilis and that gave him free access to his office. His purpose was to seek a transfer to Athens in some kind of office work so he could go to school at night. His visit left him very disappointed. After his relative had reviewed his records, he looked at Vasilis and said, "I cannot touch you. I cannot do anything. Because you are a Protestant, the army has put you in the same category with the Jehovah's Witness and the communists which were held in suspicion by the army as the enemies of the state." He advised Vasilis to go back to his base, talk with his superiors, protest his classification and request the beginning of a process to clear his name. It did not bother Vasilis that much to be called a Protestant, but association with Communists really troubled him.

Upon returning to his base, he went directly to his lieutenant, whom he knew quite well, explained to him his predicament and shared with him that he wanted to clear his name. The lieutenant brought him to his captain and his captain went with him to the office of the secret service to check his records. His captain made a recommendation to Vasilis. If he was willing to lecture in three sessions to his company and explain the differences between the Communists, Jehovah's Witnesses and the Protestants and his argument was factually convincing, they would clear his name. Vasilis readily agreed and then panicked when he realized that he had some working knowledge of the Protestants and the Jehovah's Witnesses, but he knew practically nothing of the philosophy or of the ideology of Communism, except that they were supported by the Soviet Union.

After recovering from his original shock, he remembered that there was a fellow soldier who was as red as he could get and his knowledge of the philosophy and ideology of Communism was as easy as counting 1, 2, 3. Vasilis went to him and asked him if he could teach him all that he knew about Communism. Thinking that he was having a potential convert, he did not hold anything back. He had no idea that later he would be sitting listening to Vasilis repudiating all his beliefs!

God provided the best platform that Vasilis could ever have in the army to share the word of God and his faith in Jesus Christ. Finally the captain made the arrangements for the two or three one-and-a-half-hour sessions when Vasilis was ready. He gave a brief definition of Jehovah's Witnesses, Protestantism and Communism. He proceeded to show from scripture and using Martin Luther as background to prove that Communism and Protestantism were incompatible. We do not know how many minds were changed or influenced by the presentation, but there were two or three things that took place. First, Vasilis' superiors were delighted with the presentation and speedily cleared his record, believing that there was no justification for his classification. Second, the rumor and the belief that Vasilis was working with the secret service was intensified so much that even some of his superiors began to question. It was that rumor that saved Vasilis from some hard places and difficult situations. Third and the most significant thing that took place, was the opportunity that Vasilis had to testify of the saving knowledge of Jesus Christ to his fellow soldiers and even to some of his superiors, some of which probably had never heard the gospel before.

There are a couple things more of great importance and significance that we must notice before we leave the army adventure and experience. It should be noted first that without clearing from the secret service, it would have been impossible for Vasilis to receive a Greek passport in order to travel abroad; and it would have been impossible to secure a visa for the United States. God works in all things together for good to those who love Him.

The second thing of great importance, which God used to direct Vasilis' path and future, was the youth magazine, REACH, from the Church of God. You remember, we mentioned earlier that it was sent to Vasilis from a young person in Iowa. In that magazine was a column written by Verna Joiner from Hammond, Louisiana. In that particular column she was counseling a young lady that had problems with her boyfriend. At the end of the column she ended with these words, "Do you have a problem? Write to Verna Joiner..." and gave her address. Vasilis asked himself, "Do I have a problem?" After concluding that he did not, he decided to write anyway. But two questions confronted him, "What should I write?" and "How can I write?", since Vasilis knew only a few words of the English language. He decided he was going to share his personal testimony of how he came to know Christ and with the use of a small Greek-English dictionary he spent one day and a half to write one page and two lines. Vasilis mailed the letter with preoccupation that probably Mrs. Joiner would not be able to understand it due to his poor English.

He had no idea and he never imagined the letter was directed by divine providence and that it would open the path that God had for him to follow in order to fulfill His will and purpose. Does not the scripture say that the steps of the good man are ordained from the Lord? Vasilis had put a claim on the scriptures that say, "Call upon me and I will show you wonderful and marvelous things that you have not seen before" and "Trust in the Lord with all your heart, and lean not into you own understanding; In all your ways acknowledge Him, and He will direct your path" (Prov. 3:5-6 NKJV). The fact remains for all those that trust in Him, He uses anything and everything in order to fulfill His plan for our life!

Vasilis lacked about three or four months to end his service in the Greek Army, but due to some political uncertainty in the upcoming election, his service in the army was extended another three months. This did not please him but he could not resist the inevitable. He was anxious to get out of the army and pursue the direction that God had for his life.

Finally, to his great surprise, he received a reply to his letter from Mrs. Verna Joiner. He immediately ran for his English-Greek dictionary in order to assist him in the reading of the letter. He was elated to see that his letter was understood and Mrs. Joiner expressed delight for his testimony with the promise that she would continue to pray for Vasilis. She was convinced God had a

Verna Joiner

plan for his life. Vasilis was elated and responded to her letter with a "Thank you" and some additional information that it was his intent to pursue studies for the service of the Lord wherever the Lord opened the doors. Vasilis does not recall whether there were two or three more letters exchanged with Mrs. Joiner during his military service, but in the fall of 1961 he was discharged from the army and his correspondence intensified.

A PREPARATORY TRANSITION

Upon his discharge from the Army, Vasilis spent a few days visiting with the family and then returned to Athens where he stayed with his older brother. He assisted some in the church and then worked in a clothing store of his first cousin as he endeavored to find God's direction for his life. It was a time of soul-searching, knocking on promising doors and intensifying his quest for knowledge and adventure within God's will. His story as well as his intent was known by several people, in fact by several church groups, and several possibilities seemed to appear on the horizon. There was a tense silence for a while and Vasilis had to retreat in fasting and prayer seeking divine direction, but the confidence within him was strengthened that God would open the door to the right place and at the right time. Suddenly doors began to open on the left and on the right, doors on which Vasilis never had knocked, and the challenge for him now was to discern which of these doors was from God.

The first call came from a Presbyterian Bible Institute in a city of Northern Greece called Katerini. The late Dr. Spiros Zodhiates and his brother Argos were responsible for the establishment of that Institute. But after much thought and prayer Vasilis did not feel comfortable that it was the direction God would have him to follow. So, he said, "Thank you" and declined the offer.

The second call came from a Nazarene Bible Institute in Beirut, Lebanon. How and from whom they had received information about Vasilis is not clear. The invitation was something like this, "We have heard of your story and your zeal to work for the Lord, and we would like to help you come here to study and work with us." Vasilis has no recollection of who contacted him. He was attracted to the offer but did not feel that was the direction to follow, so with a "Thank you" declined the offer.

In the meantime, Mrs. Joiner had written to Vasilis and had given him some assurance that it appeared the Lord might open the door for him to study in the United States and there were several people praying to that effect. In fact she mentioned some possibilities in her letter and that a defined response was forthcoming.

Even though it was nothing for sure, Vasilis began to muse over the possibility of going to the United States for study, but it all appeared to be a dream and he had to wait patiently to see what the Lord would do. It was during this waiting time that the unexpected took place. Vasilis received a letter from a Nazarene Bible College in Australia in which a check was enclosed to cover his traveling expenses with the invitation to study there and do work among the large number of Greek immigrants who lived there. Vasilis had no idea who had recommended him to that college. The offer created a predicament for Vasilis. This was a guarantee offered. He did not even have a promise concerning the United States, even less an offer. Even his pastor Nick Zazanis in Athens urged him to accept. He said, "It appears it might be God's will." The majority of people close to Vasilis thought it was a good idea. It could be that his good friend Takis Manetas, who had immigrated to Australia, was both studying and serving there, was the one who had recommended him.

After much thought and prayer Vasilis felt very uneasy making a decision on the affirmative and concluded that it was not God's will for him to accept their offer. He sat down and wrote a gracious letter of appreciation for their confidence and their willingness to help and shared with them that he did not feel that this was God's will for his life. He thanked them and enclosed their check in the letter. He mailed the letter not knowing what was next on God's agenda for him or what surprise was awaiting him.

Within two weeks after Vasilis had rejected the offer to go to Australia for studies, he received a letter from Mrs. Joiner stating that there was no way possible for Vasilis to come to the United States for studies. He does not recall the particular reasons stated in the letter, but it sounded definite and final. When Vasilis shared the contents of the letter with his pastor, Nick Zazanis, his response was the following, "Probably you have missed a great opportunity in your life and it is possible that you have made a mistake in not accepting the offer to go to Australia. What are you going to do now?" But Vasilis did not question his decision and he did not have second thoughts even though he was somewhat disappointed with the news. He was confident that God was working out His will in His own way and time. Therefore, he responded to brother Zazanis, "If I have made a mistake, I will have to suffer the consequences; but if God wants me to go to the United States for studies He can raise help from the stones, in spite of the fact, that the letter says there is no way for me to go to the United States for studies."

Vasilis spent many days agonizing and raising the question to the Lord, "Lord, what is the meaning of all this?" In the meantime he continued to pray, trust in the Lord and wait on Him for direction. In the Bible, a judge initially had denied the request of the poor widow, but because of her persistence, he gave in and granted it. God could touch the hearts of people thousands of miles away who held the key which could open the door for Vasilis. Days and weeks passed by which appeared that both God and people had signed off and silence was the response. But the Bible makes it clear that those who wait on the Lord would renew their strength. No matter how silent and dark the circumstances may appear and no matter how great and impossible the obstacle, God always works behind the curtains for the unfolding of His purpose and the demonstration of His power.

Vasilis does not remember how long this period of silence and waiting lasted, but he does remember the changing mood and the joy that filled his soul when a letter with the good news arrived. A second letter arrived from Mrs. Verna Joiner with totally different news from the first one. This letter stated that God had definitely opened the door for Vasilis to study at Gulf Coast Bible College (now Mid-America Christian University) in Houston, Texas. The college had agreed to accept Vasilis as a student and offered him a tuition scholarship if his grades would be above B average. The women of the First Church of God in Houston, Texas, where Dr. Max Gaulke was the pastor, had agreed to pay for the airfare. The only question that was remaining now was, would Vasilis be able to secure a passport, a visa and the necessary papers from Greece and be in the United States on time for the Fall Semester?

All the indicators were confirming he would not qualify for a student visa and the Greek Government would not grant a passport. He trusted on the Lord and he was convinced that this was God's will for his life. Therefore, he was determined to go forward leaning on the promises of God and remembering the statement that he had made before that if God wanted him to go to the States, He could raise help from the stones and He did!

Vasilis, armed with faith and the confidence that he was walking within the will of God, decided to move quickly. Because time was not his friend, he began to knock on some doors to see what God would do. First, he decided to visit the American Embassy in Athens and he asked to see the Ambassador himself. After waiting patiently for quite some time, he was ushered into his office. He was a middle-aged man with a touch of gray in his hair, blue eyes and he had a resemblance of JFK. After the introduction, the ambassador asked Vasilis, "What can I do for you?" Vasilis was nervous but confident. He decided to share his personal testimony with the ambassador, how he came to know the Lord through reading the New Testament and that he felt the Lord wanted him to study in the United States.

The Ambassador began to bombard Vasilis with questions, "What is the purpose of your studies? How long do you plan to stay in the United States? What would you do after you finish your studies? How would you support yourself?" Vasilis responded honestly and sincerely, "I want to prepare myself in order to fulfill the purpose that God has for my life. My initial request is for a visa for three years. After that I do not know. I do not know what God has planned for me after I finish my studies. I have a promise of partial scholarship from Gulf Coast Bible College, and I am confident the Lord will make a way for the rest of my support. The only thing that I know for sure right now is I want to follow God's will for my life." The ambassador was visibly moved, but both with his eyes and his questions, he was trying to validate Vasilis' sincerity. After a while he looked at Vasilis with seriousness and a resolved determination and said, "Bring me a Greek passport and I will give you a visa." Vasilis thanked him, shook hands with him and left his office.

It would be hard for others to imagine the thoughts and emotions that were raging in the mind and heart of Vasilis as he left the Embassy. There was joy in the heart and praise on his lips, knowing that God specializes on things that seem impossible.

The next step for Vasilis was the most difficult one. How could he qualify to secure a Greek passport since he did not have the proper credentials as a student? How could he secure a passport so soon, knowing that through the red tape of the Greek Government? It could take 4 to 6 months or even longer to secure one under normal circumstances. He believed that all things are possible with God. He armed himself with two photos, a birth certificate and application and decided to go to see the head man who was responsible for the issuing of passports. He sought information about the location of the building, the name of the office and the name of the individual, and he dressed appropriately for the occasion.

When he entered the building, he did not share with anyone when asked the purpose of his visit. He simply said I want to see so and so and gave the name of the individual. Later he was led into an office where he came face to face with a stern man who appeared very important and busy. "What can I do for you?" asked the man with a tone of a rushing wind in his voice. Vasilis was rather shaken by the demeanor of the man but regained his cool and decided that he was going to share his testimony what God had done in his life and why he wanted a passport. Then he shared that he had been accepted by Gulf Coast Bible College in the United States and that the American Ambassador had promised him a visa and that he needed a passport soon, if possible within a few days. The man looked at Vasilis rather impatiently and said, "No, we cannot do that. You can leave now." Vasilis smiled, thanked him politely and turned around to leave his office. He had taken a few steps when the man called him to come back. As Vasilis approached his desk, he reached in his drawer, pulled out some papers and gave them to Vasilis with these instructions, "Go to the next office, ask for so and so, and tell him that I said to issue you a passport as soon as possible." Vasilis thanked the man again, and went to the next office door as he was instructed.

In the next office Vasilis met an individual who was not in any mood for cooperation. Once he heard Vasilis' request and saw the papers that he gave him, with a raised voice he responded to Vasilis, "We cannot do that", and using words which were not very kind he said, "We have not done this for anybody else." Vasilis responded, "Don't blame me, this is what the man in the next office told me to tell you." But these words did not have any effect in changing the mood of the gentleman. About that time the superior who had heard the discussion walked in and said, "I want this passport to be finished as soon as possible." But the man replied, "We have not done this before." The superior said, "It makes no difference what we have done before, I want this passport to be finished as soon as possible", and he walked out of the office.

The gentleman looked at Vasilis and told him when to return for his passport. Vasilis thanked him and left his office. If Vasilis remembers correctly it took him a week or less to get his passport. The God who shut the lion's mouth, dried up the Red Sea, and fed a prophet by the brook, certainly He can speed up the process in issuing a passport!

Vasilis returned at the appointed time to pick up his passport as a gift from God. Then he went directly to the American Embassy where he delivered his passport. He was told to return within a couple of days and that everything would be ready for him. When he returned and stated the reason that he was there, he had the surprise of his life. The ambassador himself came out, handed him his passport, explaining to him that he had given him a visa for four years, renewable as many times as needed, and shook hands with Vasilis with these words, "God bless you and I hope you will fulfill the purpose for which you are going to the United States." The stage was set now for the adventure of faith and the exploration of the faithfulness of God, as faith and hope, expectation and trust embarked in the vastness of God's oceans of love and grace. Communications were sent to the United States that Vasilis had secured all the necessary papers and the date was set for Vasilis' departure. The preparations were intense. Vasilis' older brother made him a tailor-made suit. His sister-in-law Eleni sold something to make sure Vasilis had some money. Everyone was encouraging and participated in the preparation. Vasilis' mother had a brother who had immigrated to the United States in 1912 and she never saw him again. She was apprehensive from fear that she would not see Vasilis again. Some were sad, others joyful. Some thought Vasilis was going to the land of opportunity and others that he was crazy to go to a place he did not know and where he did not know anyone.

The last night at home, before Vasilis' departure to the United States, was emotional. Everyone had a piece of advice for Vasilis. They knew that communications were going to be difficult. Letters could take one or two months. Vasilis' father summed the whole thing up that night. He did not say much in the presence of the others (he was not a Christian at that time), but took Vasilis outside for a walk in the dark. They walked for a while without a word being exchanged. Then the father broke the silence with a choke in his voice and these words, "We know that you are going to a place that shows great promise and has a great name. We do not expect anything, we will be okay. But be sure you fulfill the purpose for which you are going." That was all he could say. They walked back home in total silence. No one knows how each one slept that night. Who could tell what the thoughts of a mother and father were? Except that everyone had surrendered to God's will and the confidence was real that the adventure of faith was in the hands of God and the expectation was that which is promised in the scripture, "You will hear a voice behind you saying, this is the way, walk ye in it"(Isaiah 30:21 KJV).

THE FLIGHT OF DESTINY

Vasilis

"The Lord said to Abraham, 'Leave your country, your people and your father's household and go to the land I will show you. I will bless those who bless you...'"

Genesis 12:1,3 (NIV)

In his preparation for the trip of his life, Vasilis spent time with his spiritual mentor, Menelaus Katsarkas, his older brother Christos, who was living in Athens at that time, and a few first cousins, Vaso, Dyonisis, Nontas and Yeota, who have been more than gracious and very hospitable to him. All gave him advice and the Zazanises both encouraged him and assured him of their prayers.

How he traveled from the village to Athens, who took him to the airport, Vasilis has no recollection whatsoever. But he does recall the warm embrace of his mother, her tears and the fact that she did not want to let him go from her arms. So, on September 7, 1962 he boarded a TWA flight from Athens to New York for an emotional and tearful departure. It was the first time in his life that he had entered in an airplane. His companions for this great flight, a small suitcase with a few clothes in it, $35.00 in his pocket, a Bible in his hands and holding on to the call and the promise that God had given to Abraham, "Get thee out of thy country, and from thy kindred, and from thy father's house, unto a land that I will shew thee: And I will make thee a great nation, and I will bless thee, and make thy name great; and thou shall be a blessing: And I will bless them that bless thee, and curse him that curseth thee: and in thee shall all families of the earth be blessed" Genesis 12:1-3 (KJV).

Of course Vasilis could not claim such a promise in its literal sense, but he claimed the spirit of the promise that God had called him; He would be with him, guide him and provide for his needs.

His seat was next to a Greek lady who was flying for the first time and appeared both nervous and anxious. By the time the airplane took off she became hysterical. Vasilis' anxiety appeared rather insignificant in the presence of the verbalization of her fears.

The trip was long and tiresome. As he continued to look out of the window, one could wonder, what emotional

127

expressions were there painted on his face? No one could tell that, but in his heart he was pondering the thoughts, "What would it be like in that place? Would there be anyone at the airport?" A host of other questions were racing through his mind. In the meantime he tried to release all the promises from the Bible that he could remember in an effort to assure himself that all would be well and that he could do all things through Christ who strengthened him.

The airplane landed in what is known now as JFK Airport in New York as darkness had begun to cover the land. As he claimed his luggage, he found himself questioning, "What do I do now? Which direction do I go for the connecting flight?" As he was pondering all these thoughts, an African-American gentleman who was working for the airport approached him and helped him to get transportation to LaGuardia Airport in order to make his connection to Houston, Texas. God always has His providential angels in the right place and at the right time. The last thing he remembers of that experience is sitting in the airport, waiting for his flight, staring outside through the glass and wondering what would be next. He was anxious to get to his destination and face the outcome no matter what it would be.

The plane landed at the Houston airport at 1:00 a.m. on Saturday. Upon claiming his luggage, an elderly gentleman made eye contact with him, which gave Vasilis the assurance that this might be the man waiting to pick him up. They were introduced to each other without either one knowing how much the other understood of the conversation. The gentleman was a dorm parent in the dorm where Vasilis was going to stay. Actually it was a two-story house with about four bedrooms upstairs and the family quarters downstairs. The trip from the airport to the college was about 45 minutes and upon arrival Vasilis was welcomed by two young men, Enrique Cepeda from Mexico and Marciano Yates from Cuba. Vasilis does not recall who had the most difficulty understanding whom, but there was one thing that warmed his heart and remained engraved in his mind. It was not just the warmth with which he was received, but the fact that all four of them knelt around the bed in his room and each one prayed in his own language, Greek, English and Spanish. Vasilis immediately became aware that the family of God has neither language nor nationality barriers.

On Saturday morning, September 8, at 10:00 a.m. Vasilis met with the Dean of the College, Dr. Walter Doty, to work out his schedule because classes were starting on Monday. Needless to say it was not the easiest meeting. The language barrier was evident. As. Dr. Doty would try to explain things to Vasilis; he would pause and look

Vasilis with his dorm parent

up at the ceiling in an apparent frustration. In the meantime Vasilis would whisper a prayer, "Lord, speak to him."

It was a year later that Vasilis learned of the meaning of Dr. Doty's staring at the ceiling. They were both at the Pollock Camp Meeting in Louisiana. If memory serves Vasilis well, he was about to speak and Dr. Doty was asked to introduce him and then the true confession came. Dr. Doty began with the words, "The first time that I met with Vasilis in my office, we had a hard time in communicating and I said to myself, 'We have made a great mistake to allow this young man to come to school without knowing the English language." Then he paused for a few moments and then continued, "I want you to know that I was wrong to think that way. Vasilis not only is doing well in school but he has been a blessing to all of us and to the whole school"

Dr. Doty, Marciano, Enrique, Vasilis and Dr. Gaulke

After Dr. Doty agreed to allow Vasilis to carry eight hours of classes the first semester, Vasilis made an unexpected request. He asked to be allowed to take evening English classes in the high school in downtown Houston. After some resistance, finally Dr. Doty agreed. Vasilis went to his room after the meeting and began to wonder how he could do all these things. So, he knelt by his bed and prayed, "Father, you have brought me to this place and you have promised to guide me and meet my needs. So, I am going to trust in you and do my best. You have promised in your word, 'My people shall not be ashamed.'"

It is difficult for Vasilis to remember much of the first days in school, except how difficult it was with the language barrier and the cultural differences. But he was sure he was in the will of God, therefore he was willing to pay any price to achieve the goal. So, he began his routine five days a week.

He would get up at five in the morning, have his devotions and then get ready for school. At noon he would go to the cafeteria, have lunch, and about 1:30 in the afternoon he would catch the bus and go to the high school for his English classes. He would return to his room about 10:00 p.m., study some and then go to bed, ready to repeat the routine the next day.

His life and encouragement were aided by his friendship with Enrique Cepeda, with whom he would spend time in prayer, and by the assistance of Dr. Robert Bland who was teaching a discipleship class early in the morning which Vasilis had joined. It was those relationships and others that greatly influenced his life where he was exposed to scriptural memorization and service as well as to spiritual tools for growth and witness. It was that class and the leadership of Dr. Bland that equipped Vasilis for Christian service in the college and ignited the fire of evangelism in his soul as he began to travel on the weekend in different meetings.

Vasilis had assumed more responsibility than he should have in the first six months in his new surroundings. There was no time left for anything else, except attending church services and serve occasionally somewhere. The pressure was building in such a way that at night while he would lay down in the bed, he would feel as if the bed was going around and around and then the thought would enter his mind, "You thought that God has brought you here for a purpose, you are going to get crazy and you will be an embarrassment to yourself, to the faith that you claim, to your family and everyone else." The only way Vasilis could combat such thoughts was to get up and engage in prayer and claiming the promises of God, specially the one from Hosea, "And my people shall not be ashamed" (Joel 2:27 KJV).

Vasilis had made the journey by faith and he was trusting on the Lord, but he had little knowledge and no concrete arrangements on how his financial needs were going to get met. He knew that he could charge his meals during the week in the cafeteria. You should have seen his facial expressions one day when they told him that they had hot dogs for supper. But his $35.00 did not last long and the cafeteria was closed on the weekends. So after church on some Sundays, Vasilis would take a walk to a park that was close by the school and then return to his room and have a couple glasses of water. Partially because of pride and because of his declared faith that God would provide, he did not let anyone know about his situation. He was convinced of two things, that God always honors faith and that He answers prayer. God knew his name, He knew where he was and He was aware of all his needs, and he would always make reference to the *scripture that the angel of the Lord encampeth around about those who fear Him.*

He had not become fully aware that God had dispatched more than one angel, not angels with wings and halos, but angels in the form of human beings who had discernment and who were sensitive to the Spirit of God. A few times a white envelop would show up in Vasilis' mail box with a few dollars in it – no name, no message and no indication whatsoever. God continued to surprise Vasilis in different ways, but the most impressive was during the first Christmas at the school.

The Christmas vacation was scheduled to begin on Thursday at noon. Most of the students, with the exception of a few who worked, would be leaving for home and the cafeteria was going to be closed for the duration of the Christmas vacation, about 10 days. Vasilis had no plans to go anywhere and he had no money. No one knew his situation; at least he thought no one knew. On Wednesday evening before he went to bed, he decided to have a frank conversation with the Lord in prayer. He prayed, "Lord, tomorrow begins the Christmas vacation and most of the students will be going home, but Your Bill has no home to go to and the cafeteria will be closed and he has no money. You have brought me here and you have promised to provide for my needs. Thank you for your faithfulness and for the promises of your word."

Vasilis went to bed and in the morning to school as he did every day. At 11:55 a.m. the last bell for classes rang and the hallways were filled with the noise of happy laughter and smiling faces. Everyone was rushing to get out of the building. Vasilis walked slowly to his mail box where he had the surprise of his life. There was a large white envelope with his name on it from the International Bank. Inside the envelope was a check as large as the envelope. Vasilis does not recall the amount, but that is irrelevant because it was enough to meet his present needs. No name and no message or place of origin. Even to this day Vasilis has no knowledge of who God used to meet his needs except that God had kept His promises.

But God had not finished yet. He had another surprise for Vasilis. Paul and Kathy Bentley, from New Albany, Indiana, were going home for the break. They knew Vasilis had some distant relatives he had never met in Gary, Indiana. They decided to ask Vasilis to go and spend Christmas with them and they would make an effort to stop by Gary so he could meet his relatives. God had covered all bases. The trip was enjoyable, the fellowship with all the people great and the meeting of Vasilis with his relatives proved to be rewarding and opened doors for future ministry. God never makes mistakes!

The policy of the school was that if a foreign student had a grade above B average that he/she could have tuition scholarship. Vasilis was able to achieve such a goal the first nine weeks of the first semester. Later he secured a part time job with the school where the proceeds were applied toward his school bill. Even though the first year had many obstacles and some difficulties, overall it proved to be a good year and Vasilis had integrated quite well in the college community. He enjoyed warm relationships, remained focused and worked hard to accomplish his goal. Before the end of the first school year, the student body voted Vasilis the most outstanding student of the year, which came as a great surprise to him. As a response to such an honor, he called the student body to a day of fasting and prayer which was received with great response.

GOD MAPS THE FUTURE

As the first school year came to an end, Vasilis had begun to receive invitations for speaking, and it appeared God was mapping out the future. He traveled to Baton Rouge, Louisiana, for a speaking engagement. Then a couple gave him a ride to Hammond, Louisiana, where he met for the first time Verna and Charles Joiner. Verna was the lady that was praying for Vasilis and responsible for beginning the process so Vasilis could come to the United States for study. Their reunion was warm and they accepted Vasilis as if he was their son, and their guidance and counsel proved very helpful. Together with the Joiners, Vasilis traveled to Meridian, Mississippi, where Mrs. Joiner had scheduled him to speak at the Park View Church of God. There they were entertained by the family of Charles Shumate. In fact Charles surrendered his bed that evening so Vasilis could have a place to sleep. He has been saying through the years that Charles turned out to be so good because he gave his bed to a man of God for one evening! No one could envision that later Charles and Vasilis would be neighboring pastors and they would exchange pulpits. It was a memorable night at the Shumate house as several got together in the back yard and fellowshipped around watermelon.

The journey continued to Tennessee where they visited Brother Starkey's church and then continued the journey to Anderson Camp Meeting. Vasilis was greatly moved by the size, the warmth and the spirit of the convention. He was scheduled by Sister Joiner to speak to the women's meeting in the old gym and he attended early prayer meeting where sister Ethel used to sing, "I'll fly away". He met several Greeks from Chicago, Gary, Indiana, and Detroit, Michigan. He made several new friends and the Lord began to open doors for the whole summer.

One day, during the convention, while at the Anderson Hotel in downtown Anderson, Vasilis had an encounter with a wonderful couple, Don and June Alexander, from Oak Hill, West Virginia. They were part of a singing group called Sing Time Quartet. They were God-sent in the life of Vasilis. Not only did they become lifetime friends, but they were helpful to him in many ways. The women of their church, Jones Avenue Church of God, took him as a missions project while he was in school. He was invited to speak at their church both when John Winters and Phil Houser were their pastors. Their home became Vasilis' home while in speaking engagements in West Virginia. Vasilis always speaks with great appreciation about them and he is grateful for their unselfish spirit and hospitality.

That summer took Vasilis to several states and cities, giving him the opportunity to get a good feel of life and the culture of the United States and enhancing his life. In the meantime God was using him to minister to people and touch lives with the message of God's word. As the

Don and June Alexander

summer was coming to a close, Vasilis found himself speaking at the Church of God in New Orleans. Fom there he flew to Detroit, Michigan to speak to the convention of the Greek Church of God. It was the highlight for Vasilis that summer. There he met several elderly Greeks and the leadership of the church such as John Pappas, Restos, Karamitros, Tsonos and others. It was brother Restos later who took Vasilis' articles and published them in the Greek Gospel Trumpet. There he met also three elderly Greek sisters who were prayer warriors for him and maintained correspondence with him while in school, Agnes, Bessie Angelos and sister Commondurou.

136

He returned to school in September, elated with the way that God had led, grateful for the way He had blessed and met his needs; and thankful that God had showered him with so many new friends who began to get involved both in his education and ministry. There is something that Vasilis learned that summer. None of us is self-made or self-sufficient. We are all the product of God's grace and what His grace had provided through other people in order to enhance both our life and ministry. Nehemiah had a vision and a burden to rebuild the walls of Jerusalem, but God touched the heart of kings and a host of other people to help him accomplish the task. None of us travels alone in life. It might be a raven, an angel, a widow or a tent maker, but all of us get that helping hand in everything that we do for the glory of God and the advancement of His kingdom.

A BIRD'S EYEVIEW OF VASILIS' LIFE AND MINISTRY WHILE IN SCHOOL

He began his second year full of enthusiasm and with great anticipation. His studies progressed well and his ministry began to expand both in the campus and the surrounding area. Two of the students, which went with him quite often, were his roommate, Edgar Martin, and his good friend, Enrique Cepeda. He could not be thankful enough for the warmth and support of the college family and the acceptance and support of the church. Soon he was elected president of his class, president of the Missions Club and one of the leaders of the Christian Service program of the college. The Christian Service program engaged in two-by-two visitation, conducted Bible studies at homes and Vacation Bible schools in poor neighborhoods.

Dr. Max Gaulke was President of Gulf Coast Bible College and pastor of the 11th Street Church of God in Houston. He also was Vasilis' homiletics professor and had a great impact on his life and ministry. He bestowed one of the greatest honors on Vasilis by expressing confidence in him and inviting him after he had returned from his summer preaching schedule to preach for him on Sunday evenings. Dr. Gaulke had a great impact on him with his passion for the Word and his expository preaching. He kept in touch with Vasilis throughout his ministry till just two or three years before his death. He visited him in his places of service and corresponded with him at least twice a year.

Dr. David Gaulke, former missionary to China and Kenya, was Vasilis' professor of missions, both in class and outside the class. Vasilis always had a vision of the church at large and its mission around the world. In fact, soon after his conversion he was dreaming of becoming a missionary to Africa. Dr. David Gaulke both intensified that passion and gave it a Biblical perspective. During the Holy Week the college church was conducting nightly services. On Thursday evening was the celebration of the Lord's Supper and foot washing. Vasilis never had experienced or participated in a foot washing service before. As the service progressed, Dr. David Gaulke knelt before Vasilis in preparation to wash his feet. He does not recall a word that Dr. David said, but he never can erase the expression of his face and the tears that ran down his cheeks. It was like the angel of the Lord or better, like the Lord Jesus Christ was ministering to Vasilis.

Vasilis recalls vividly that at a chapel service where Dr. David Gaulke had shared the challenge of missions, he responded to the invitation. While kneeling next to Vasilis, he asked him, "Vasilis, what can we pray about?" Vasilis responded, "I feel so inadequate." It was his response that sealed the deal for Vasilis. With moisture in his eyes and a choke in his voice he said, "Vasilis, none of us is adequate, but the grace of God is sufficient and He will enable us to do what He has for us." That year he had the privilege to travel to a Missions Convention with Dr. Gaulke to Monroe, Louisiana, and share the pulpit with him. This is what Vasilis says concerning that trip, "I have learned more about the spirit of missions during that trip, than I have learned from all the classes that I have taken and all the books that I have read." In 1975-76, while Vasilis was a missionary candidate, Dr. Gaulke was a member of the Missionary Board and when he saw Vasilis for an interview, he dove across the room and greeted him with the warmest embrace. Examples are more powerful than any words.

Dr. Walter Doty, Dean of the college, was also a professor of theology. His wisdom and gentleness, combined with his counsel and the warm hospitality of him and his wife, had proven to be a sustaining force for Vasilis' college years.

Dr. Donald Brumfield, speech, drama and Christian Education professor, was Vasilis' constant encourager and helper. He was one of the best listeners when Vasilis would return to the campus after he had ministered somewhere during the weekend. If he had heard anything about the outcome of the meeting, he would always drop a note in Vasilis' mail box like this one that was found in his box a long time ago, "Dear Bill: The good word of your ministry over the weekend has reached my ears. I rejoice that you have, once again, humbled yourself unto the service of God through the Holy Spirit. My prayer for you is Hebrews 13:20-21. In Christ's love, Donald Brumfield" (1964).

Dr. Robert Bland, professor of English and Spanish, as well as head of the Christian service of the college, had a great impact on Vasilis, especially in the area of discipleship. His early morning discipleship class and sessions of prayer, combined with the warm hospitality in his home with his wife, proved to make a lasting mark on Vasilis life.

The list would be very long if Vasilis would endeavor to describe the ways that the personnel of Gulf Coast Bible College influenced his life, but it will suffice here to mention a few names: Dr. Kenneth Jones, Dr. Evert Carver, Dr. William McDonald, Dr. Robert Adams, Dr. Nelson Trick and Dr. Ruth Kirk.

In addition to the college personnel, there was a network of students with whom Vasilis related in different levels and who had impacted his life. Among the many were his roommate, Edgar Martin, and his good friend, Enrique Cepeda. Vasilis recalls when George Golden arrived in the campus as a student. He had a speech impediment and a heavy accent. So, Vasilis asked, "What country is he from?" Everyone was humored with his question, but when the response came, "from Alabama", he was greatly embarrassed.

In the last three years of Vasilis' schooling the Lord continued to open doors for ministry, not only during the school breaks, but throughout the year. His initial states of ministry were Texas, Louisiana, Indiana, Illinois, Ohio, Kentucky, West Virginia, Tennessee and Virginia.

The house of Charles and Verna Joiner, who were responsible for Vasilis coming to the United States, was a frequent stop for Vasilis and always felt like home. There he found wise counsel, faith, acceptance, encouragement and warm hospitality. Sister Verna treated him better than a son! Being an author, she prompted Vasilis with a lot of questions and then later she wrote his story in an abbreviated form in the Sunday School Times and later it appeared in the Junior High Sunday School Quarterly of the Church of God for two sessions. All her children, Marie, Lynda, Joyce, Howard and Herb, had accepted Vasilis as part of the family. It is almost ironic that later two of her daughters visited Vasilis' family in Greece and spent time with them. Knowing the contribution that they had made in Vasilis' family, they were treated as if they were angels from God.

Verna's confidence and faith in Vasilis were unshakable. Every time Vasilis had a speaking engagement within 60 miles driving distance from her home, both she and her husband would attend. One time when Vasilis was speaking in the area, she attended three services on the same day but in different churches. In the evening after they had returned home she commented with a smile, "I wish those dry bones would rise up so we can move on to something else and away from the valley of dry bones!" What a people! What a spirit! What a love, confidence and trust! It is people like these that are placed in our path by God in order to help us fulfill His purpose in our journey.

Vasilis never anticipated that God, who took him out of a mountainous and remote village in Greece and brought him to the most modern and prosperous nation on the face of the earth, that He would introduce him to the mountains of West Virginia. He had ministered a lot in that state and met some of the most loving and hospitable people, some of whom became a permanent fixture in Vasilis' life and ministry. The scripture was fulfilled when Jesus said he who leaves father and mother, brother and sister for my sake shall receive them a hundred-fold back.

Don and June Alexander with their three children Greg, Tommy and Steve, were the first from that state that Vasilis met, excluding Nilah Basham, whom he had met in Greece. Their home was Vasilis' base while in West Virginia. Their church was both hospitable and supportive to Vasilis, and the president of the women's group, Sister Greene, kept correspondence with him while in school. Don and June, together with the Sing Time Quartet, put a lot of miles and sacrificed a lot to be helpful to Vasilis during those years. What a people! What a love and acceptance! Probably we will meet them again somewhere in the journey.

Leon Nunley was pastoring a small church in Welch, West Virginia, when he first invited Vasilis to preach at his church. How Vasilis got there is not clear. Later he moved to Fayetteville, West Virginia, and became the pastor of the First Church of God. He not only opened his heart, his home and his pulpit to Vasilis for frequent preaching engagements, but later his congregation would become the number one provider of support for Vasilis for four years while on the mission field. It was Leon Nunley that introduced Vasilis to four people in his congregation with whom Vasilis developed family-like relationships and who proved to be a blessing from God and who had a great impact on Vasilis' life and ministry for years. Vasilis' testimony, faith and commitment challenged them so much that immediately they opened their hearts and homes to him. They were Charles and Joyce Payne, and Charles' parents, Donald and Velma Payne. They had a funeral home business in that town.

Charles and Vasilis became close like brothers. It was Charles that taught Vasilis one of the hardest lessons that he had to learn. During his Seminary studies, Vasilis had scheduled a series of nine days meeting in the surrounding area where Charles was living. Each evening he had a meeting in a different church. Some of the time he stayed with the Paynes and the other time with the Alexanders. During that stay, Charles noticed that Vasilis did not have enough clothes to change suits for the different services. So one day he took Vasilis to a rack where about three dozen suits were hanging and asked Vasilis to select two or three suits because Vasilis needed them. Vasilis resisted and his pride caused him great embarrassment. His reply was, "I do not need any suits. I am doing fine." Charles was both patient and wise; he did not push the issue, but rather invited Vasilis to his office to get something to drink. As they sat down Charles looked Vasilis straight in the eyes and asked him some pointed questions. "Do you enjoy what you are doing? Do you enjoy preaching the word and having people come to know the Lord? Do you enjoy encouraging people and helping them in their walk with the Lord? Do you receive a blessing and does it make you feel good when people are helped?" Vasilis responded to all the questions with an affirmative, "YES", but he was not prepared for the question that was going to follow. Charles leaned forward in his chair and in some way he asserted his authority and in a strong voice asked Vasilis, "Has it ever dawned on you that we too have a ministry, even though somewhat difference than yours, and that we too want to feel that we are contributing to the kingdom of God? We too want to feel good and be blessed! Why are you so proud that you will not allow us to do our ministry in order to help your ministry and be blessed?" Wow! What a rebuke! What lesson! The only thing that Vasilis could say, "I am sorry. I will take two suits!"

It was somewhere during that time Vasilis' journey took him to Craigsville Camp Meeting in West Virginia. That place has a great significance for Vasilis because it was there he met his wife-to-be, as we shall see later. There he met the pastor of the First Church of God in Cottle, West Virginia, which was across the road from the camp meeting. He was a well-built, redheaded, blue-eyed, light-complexioned individual with a thundering voice, spoke with authority and it appeared that he did not fear anything. For those who would like to put labels on people, probably they would have called him ultra-conservative and probably negative. For him there was nothing between. "You either are or ain't" to use his words. His authority and the demeanor made you feel guilty, even if you were not. His name was Ray Wyant.

When Ray heard Vasilis' testimony he invited Vasilis to share with his church. After that day a long-lasting relationship was established with him, his wife Virginia, and their two children, Lynn and Thomas. Ray befriended Vasilis and quite often referred to him in the early years as "Little Paul". Later when Vasilis came to know Ray quite well, he said this about him, "Behind that thunderous, authoritative voice

Rev. Ray Wyant

and stern look, I discovered a heart that was melting with love for God, His church and the truth of His word, and with a keen and sacrificial interest for missions." Their kindness, support and the continuous freedom to minister to their congregation covers a period of 45 years. He has been a true friend and supporter of Vasilis' missionary adventures and he made some things possible which at the time appeared impossible. That is the power of the Gospel. This is the spirit of Christ, that will take people of different backgrounds, different personalities and temperaments and merge them in the unity of the Spirit of Christ and put an inscription over them, "Behold, how they love one another" and "Love covers a multitude of sins!"(1 Peter 4:8 NKJV).

WHEN THE LIGHTS ALMOST GO OUT

Vasilis' faith was strong and his commitment firm. When there were some low points of discouragement and questioning, he would engage vigorously in the fight of faith and claim the promises of God and rely on His faithfulness. One should not get the impression that Vasilis' last three years in school were free of challenges and crises. One should be aware that communications with the family were slow and far between. They could communicate only with letters and transit and delivery took a long time. Someone in Greece could die and it would have taken, sometimes, more than a month for Vasilis to get the news. Vasilis did not know what was happening to the family or the family what was happening to Vasilis. Especially when Vasilis would get involved with his studies, he became somewhat neglectful in writing (something that he has regretted tremendously). He had missed a lot of joyful and sad things in the family.

There were times he felt all alone, with no one to share his fears or challenges. During those times he resorted into prolonged prayer, reminding God of His promises and claiming His faithfulness. The hymn, "Alone With God" had become his constant companion, especially in the evening hours. The psalms that deal with a variety of human emotions and with many of the events of life had become his refuge; and quite often he would repeat, "As the hart panteth after the water brooks, so my soul thirsteth for God" (Ps. 42:1). Vasilis recalls there was a time when he had not received news from the family for quite some time. He was preoccupied and concerned. After his class that day as he passed by his mailbox, he found a letter from his oldest brother. He ran with it toward the cafeteria so he would not be too far behind in the line. As he was waiting to get closer and pick up his tray, he decided to open the letter and began to read, "My beloved brother Bill, Today we have been thinking of you and decided to write a few lines and greet you. Everyone in the family send you their love, Mother, father, Christos, Yeota and the children with the exception of Eleni (that is his wife). She is not able to greet you because the other evening suddenly left us and went to be with the Lord…" Vasilis was overtaken with emotion. He turned around and went back to his room. It was so difficult not to be able to talk with anyone in the family.

There was another event that took place just a few months before his graduation from college. There was a reviewing committee which had visited the college in preparation for renewing its accreditation. While in the dean's office they asked to see the files of some of the students. The dean knew Vasilis had good grades, so he pulled out his file and gave it to the committee. As they reviewed his file, they noticed that there was no high school transcript. They asked for an explanation and the dean replied, "We do not have one. He did not make one available to us." Their response, firm and final, "He cannot graduate without the proper high school documentation, no matter how good grades he has." When the dean informed Vasilis of the predicament it had both a serious note and a humorous one. Here you had a student who was about to graduate from college summa cum laud and he was asking how could he get a high school diploma quickly? So he went to the high school where he had taken English evening classes and shared with them his dilemma. "How can I get a high school diploma quickly?" They assured him he could take a battery of tests and if he passed them they would give him a diploma equivalent to high school. They set the week for the test and Vasilis had the week of his life. Some of the materials that he was tested on, if he was not a Greek, he would have said, "It is all Greek to me!" But since he was a Greek, the only thing that he could say, "I have no idea what they are talking about."

He did his best and then waited for the results. When he received the results he could not tell whether he or his

English professor was more excited because his percentile was so high. Vasilis could not interpret the results but his professor helped him understand their meaning. The Bible says that when God is pleased with a man, He makes even his enemies to be friendly with him. The songwriter says, "Jesus never fails," and the promise of God is, "My people shall not be ashamed" (Joel 2:27 KJV).

He also was selected to respond to the charges that were given to the graduates. The commencement speaker was Dr. Robert Nicholson from Anderson, Indiana, and the charges were given by Dr. Everett Carver.

As this chapter of the journey was coming to a close, the hand of God had begun to draw the diagrams for the next chapter. Vasilis, with a sense of amazement, gratitude and contentment, had begun to envision the next chapter; he was musing over the words of the hymn, "God leads His children along, some through the waters, some through the flood, some through great sorrow, but all through the blood", and then, "To God be the glory, great things He has done!"

GOD PROVIDES A PARTNER
FOR LIFE AND MINISTRY

Kay and Vasilis

"Whoso findeth a wife findeth a good thing, and obtaineth favour of the Lord"

Proverbs 18:22 (KJV).

Vasilis spent all his summers and vacations during his college years traveling as an evangelist in Missions Conventions, revival meetings, camp meetings and youth conventions. The summer of 1965 was going to bring a different turn. After Anderson Camp Meeting, known now as the North American Convention, he was invited to speak to the youth at the Craigsville Camp Meeting in West Virginia, and then he had made a commitment to spend the rest of the summer helping the Greek Church of God in Gary, Indiana. He was excited about both possibilities, two or three months among Greeks and among some distant relatives who were part of the church. That was a treat. He could not wait to get there.

He arrived at the Craigsville Camp Meeting with Don and June Alexander who were serving as his hosts. While in camp meeting they had made arrangements for Vasilis to stay at someone's house next to the campground. The owners were on vacation. As he walked into the campground, he noticed that a young lady was coming down the steps from the cabins, carrying a basin of water. She had on a blue skirt and white blouse, long hair with curls, blue eyes, a pleasant smile and an innocence painted all over her face. Vasilis' heart skipped a beat and he said to himself, "That is the girl!"

Later while he walked in the tabernacle with the Alexanders, they introduced him to a group of people, sitting on the second bench from the front. Again Vasilis had the surprise of his life. Among the people to whom he was introduced were Rev. Frank Ramey and his wife Lillian and next to them was the gorgeous young lady named Kay. It was the same young lady that he had seen coming down the steps. There were a few moments of conversation of which Vasilis recalls absolutely nothing, except that at one point of the conversation, he looked at Kay and said, "At six o'clock this evening I will be giving my testimony in the youth meeting, and I would like for you to sing the song, "It Took A Miracle of Love and Grace". To his surprise, she agreed and she did an excellent job. The song introduced what the grace of God had done in Vasilis' life.

It was during that service that an eye contact was made that gave the confirmation that through all these, the Lord might have a plan. The next day Vasilis had one-on-one conversation with Kay and he took the courage to invite her to dinner in a small nearby restaurant. Since he did not have transportation and the Greyhound Bus was his summer transportation, the Alexanders volunteered to drop by and pick them up thirty minutes before the evening service. Both of them were somewhat nervous and it seemed they looked at the menu forever in trying to make a choice. They were each waiting on the other to take the initiative and make the choice. So finally, Vasilis, seeing that the most expensive thing on the menu was pork chops, made the suggestion to which Kay readily agreed. The funny thing about this is that later they admitted to each other that neither one of them like pork chops! Vasilis thinks he ordered the pork chops because it was the most expensive thing on the menu and he wanted to make a good impression.

So it was over a dinner of pork chops that neither liked nor neither ate, that God sealed their destiny and the enjoyable journey began. The Alexanders picked them up at the appointed time and returned for the evening service. Since Kay was going to return to her home the next day, telephone numbers and addresses were exchanged and they said their good-byes. Upon returning to Gary, Indiana, Vasilis maintained consistent correspondence with Kay and there were a few telephone calls exchanged.

When Vasilis arrived in Gary, Indiana, for his internship with the Greek Church of God, he was assigned to lodge in the house of a distant aunt named Bessie Angelos, a lady that loved the Lord and had the sweetest disposition and warm spirit of hospitality. She had two daughters and a son named Vanges. Mary was married to Nick Eliopoulos who had come from

Greece and together with Vanges, started the ELLAS Construction Company. Christina was married to Nick Petsas who was a builder. Vasilis states that it would be difficult to put in words the impact that that summer had on his life and ministry and the spirit with which both the relatives and the church treated him. It was one of the most rewarding experiences either way you measure it.

The Greek Church of God in Gary was conducting all its services in Greek with the exception of English language Sunday school for the children. It was natural that the main services would be attended primarily by older folks who understood Greek. Vasilis met with the leadership of the church and suggested a schedule that could meet the needs of all. Sunday school classes would be in English and during that time Vasilis would have a service in Greek in the sanctuary. Sunday morning and Sunday evening services would be in English. Wednesday would be a preaching service in Greek. To the amazement and surprise of all, every one responded positively and the church experienced revitalization both in spirit and in numbers. It was a refreshing time for Vasilis and gave him the opportunity to get acquainted with the Greek community both in Gary and in Chicago and several leaders of the Greek Church.

Nick and Vanges wanted to help Vasilis cope with his school expenses when he returned to school. Therefore, they hired him as a flag boy in their construction company, four days a week. This proved to be a gift from God. Christina and Mary made sure that upon returning to school, Vasilis would not lack anything. Their shopping for him was an extravaganza that Vasilis had never seen before. He was both grateful and thankful for such an expression of love and thoughtfulness. One of the most rewarding things during that time was the daily prayer time he had with his aunt Bessie. What a sweet lady; she did spoil Vasilis with her Greek cooking that summer. Is it not amazing how God places the right people in the right place in order to meet needs and help us fulfill His purpose?

Vasilis returned to Houston the first week of September 1965 in order to finish his last year of college. He merged into his studies with eagerness and determination, keeping his eyes on the goal. But he always took time to keep his courtship going by mail and phone calls. The relationship was serious but from a distance, and certain plans were set into motion. Vasilis thought about flying to Kay's house during Christmas to meet all her family, ask for permission and make definite plans, but before he could do that, in order to comply with the school rules, he had to have the college's permission. He had a personal meeting with the President, Dr. Max Gaulke, and upon receiving permission; he made the definite plans for the visit.

So, during the Christmas vacation in December 1965, armed with an engagement ring, a gift and a lot of mixed feelings of expectation, he boarded a plane from Houston, Texas to Cleveland, Ohio. There Kay picked him up and they made the 45-minute trip to meet her family. He received a warm welcome and outstanding hospitality. After a couple days, Vasilis mastered enough courage to ask permission from Mr. Walter Matney to marry his daughter. Vasilis does not recall if he said an out loud, "yes", but he was sure he did not say "no". From that time things were set into forward positive motion. Vasilis visited Kay's family again on Easter 1966, and it was during that time the definite plans were made and date was set for the wedding.

In May 1966 Vasilis graduated from Gulf Coast Bible College and immediately began his speaking engagements for the summer with most of the time spent with the church in West Virginia, which has proven to be very hospitable to Vasilis. Just a couple or three weeks before the wedding, he had a revival meeting with his friend Ray Wyant at the Cottle Church of God, which proved to be rewarding in more than one way.

The irony of the whole thing during this time was the fact that Vasilis was planning to get married, take on the responsibility of a wife, but he had no idea what he was going to do afterward. He had no job; no place to live, and no definite direction. Was this a sign of a foolish Greek or a sign of unusual faith and trust? The only things he had to his name was $1,500, a few clothes and books, and a small car which his friend, Charles Payne, had helped him to buy. When Vasilis is asked about it, his reply is, "I cannot believe I did that and that she would marry me without knowing what we were going to do!" Love does a lot of strange things and sometimes foolish ones. Is it not wonderful that sometimes God uses even our ignorance to fulfill His purpose?

The date for the wedding was set for August 27, 1966 at the Elyria Church of God. Rev. C.N. Watson, Kay's former pastor was to officiate; Edgar Martin, Vasilis' roommate was going to be the best man. Kay's three sisters would serve as the bridesmaids and Vasilis had invited the Sing Time Quartet to do the singing. He does not recall all that were planning to attend the ceremony or all those who were going to participate, but there was one thing that was laying heavy on his mind. None of his family would be able to share such a joyful occasion with him. But his cousins from Gary and Munster, Indiana, Mary and Christina, knowing that Vasilis did not have any family in the United States, were not about to allow such an occasion to take place without any Greek flavor in it. So they prepared what is called in Greek, mbabounieras, sugar-coated almonds in different colors, wrapped in white veil cloth and tied with a nice ribbon which was distributed to the attendees.

He finished his speaking engagements a week before the ceremony and then headed for Lorain, Ohio, for the final preparations. The ceremony proceeded quite well. After the reception as darkness began to cover the little church in Elyria, Vasilis and Kay got into their little car and sped out into the night without any clear direction in mind where they were going. Finally about 2:00 a.m. they stopped at a countryside motel and asked for a room. The man who attended them was a middle-aged man with dark hair and a mustache of Italian descent. When he was informed that they just have been married, he got all excited and said, "I have something special for you without an extra charge" and gave them the keys to a beautiful suite. Have you ever started on a honeymoon without knowing where you were going, without a place to stay and without a place to come back to or a job? It seems rare and foolish, doesn't it? But the journey of faith has many adventures which to many people appears foolishness and upon reflection, they even frighten those who have lived them.

The honeymoon was adventurous and eventful. Four days in a motel with car trouble, a long trip to the dealership to change cars, a long trip to Houston, Texas to introduce the bride to the college community and gather the few belongings that Vasilis had left there, and then a return to Gary, Indiana. In the absence of definite direction from the Lord, they thought that it might be wise to rent an apartment in a familiar environment until they had a specific direction. They would be close to people that they knew and since they could render some services to the Greek Church there, it made sense to them.

They located a small apartment for which the lady was asking two months' deposit. But Kay objected to it and said, "No, one month's rent for deposit is sufficient." They paid the first month's rent and the deposit and began cleaning and preparing the place to move in. On the second or third day the house was almost ready for the move, when a gentleman appeared rather upset and said, "What are you doing in my apartment?" When they informed him that they had rented it from a lady, his response was, "This is my apartment and she has no authority to rent it to any one, you get out!" The lady was his ex-wife who took the money and disappeared. Here they were, Vasilis and Kay, had spent most of their money, had cleaned the place up and now they had no place to stay!

Some would view such an experience and say, "Bad judgment." Others would look at it and say, "Bad luck." There is no doubt there will be others who would come up with some choice words to describe such an experience or Vasilis and Kay's judgment. But are there not times when we are committed to do God's will and we are faithful in what we know to be His will, that God can take bad experiences and turn them to a blessing? Is it not true that God works in all things together for good to those who love Him? You see divine providence directs our path. In the case of Vasilis and Kay, God allowed this to happen in order to focus on a direction that they were not willing to focus, and they had been somewhat resistant.

Either in May or the early part of June of that year, Vasilis was invited to speak at the First Church of God in Kankakee, Illinois. The church wanted to consider Vasilis as their pastor, but he would not give his consent for a vote. During the summer the church had tried several prospects but would not accept (with the excuse as Vasilis and Kay learned later), saying, "We would like to have that Greek young man for our pastor." Vasilis and Kay had no such awareness of what was going on in the church.

It was during that eventful time in Vasilis and Kay's journey, that Mr. Cassidy, chairman of the board from the church of Kankakee, called Vasilis to ask if he would consider to come and preach for them the following Sunday. Vasilis was quick to respond that he was not interested in becoming the pastor of the church. Mr. Cassidy responded, "I know that, but you can come and preach for us, the people would like to hear you again." Vasilis and Kay went the following Sunday and enjoyed a very warm service; but at the close of the service the church had planned to take a vote without Vasilis' knowledge or consent. The vote was taken so quickly that Vasilis did not have time to even object. It was 100 per cent and the chairman, a gracious, loving man with character and integrity, looked at Vasilis and said, "You see, the Lord wants you to be our pastor." Vasilis still resisted but after a week of prayer, he could not resist anymore. He thought it might be God opening the door as the first step toward the longer journey of faith.

It became evident later that it was God's will for them to be in that place at that time. While there, almost a year, Vasilis and Kay drove to Gary, Indiana each Thursday evening to preach to the Greek Church of God there in Greek. In fact, Vasilis remembers with great joy that some of his first converts in Kankakee were Takes Eliopoulos and Jim Petsas, his cousins' sons who had come with the family for a visit in a worship service. It was not only that the place provided a multifaceted ministry, but it appeared to be a nurturing place to shape their life for what God had planned ahead in the journey.

There were mountaintops and low valleys. There were moments of singing and moments of sighing. It was during those difficult and trying moments that Kay proved to be the most valuable partner in life and ministry. Her steady faith and unwavering commitment to the truth, combined with her love for the Lord and the genuine spirit of stewardship, made her a source of strength for Vasilis. It was there that one Sunday morning after returning to the parsonage from the Sunday morning service, Kay had sensed Vasilis' discouragement. There is no recollection of anything unusual that had taken place in the service or what had caused the discouragement. But when they walked in the living room, she threw both arms around Vasilis' neck and began to sing, *Do you have any rivers that seem impossible to cross, any mountains that you cannot tunnel through? God specializes on things that are impossible, what He has done for others, He will do the same for you.* It was that kind of attitude that kept the focus and turned the place to the habitation of God with an overflow of His peace and presence.

A NEW SAIL OF FAITH
FROM KANKAKEE TO ASBURY

First Church of God, Kankakee, Illinois

"I lift up my eyes to the hill – where does my help come from?
My help comes from the Lord, the maker of heaven and earth"
Psalm 121:1-2 (NIV).

Even though Vasilis and Kay's pastoral experience of the small church in Kankakee was a positive one and they enjoyed their involvement with the Greek Church in Gary and Chicago, there was restlessness in both of them. There was a desire for continuous education, a burden for missions and evangelism, and a greater outlet for ministry. There was a desire not to settle for the mediocre and the feeling that there was something else more in which they should be engaging.

In was decided, after much thought, reflection and prayer, that they should go back to school by faith and do evangelistic work as the Lord would open doors and opportunities. But where could they go? There were two choices before them at that time, Anderson School of Theology or Asbury Seminary. Vasilis was influenced a great deal by the writings of Dr. Robert Coleman. He visited both schools, but after spending considerable time with Dr. Trainer, Dean of Asbury Seminary, he concluded Asbury was the place for them. Vasilis could attend Seminary and Kay Asbury College. After receiving the notice that both of them were accepted, they began the preparations for the transition.

As they were making preparation to leave the pastorate by the end of December and notified the church, they were not aware a surprise was in the making. It was during that time Vasilis received a telephone call from his friend, Ray Wyant, from West Virginia, with the strangest question, "Do you have your passports ready?" Vasilis, being surprised by such question asked, "Why?" The reply came, "Because you are going to Greece for Christmas. The church and some friends had bought the tickets and they want you to go to Greece and you can get back in time to start classes in January." Vasilis knew that you never win an argument with Ray Wyant!

Even though the time was short, they were able to secure their passports on time, move their few things to the Asbury Seminary's apartment, load their 1965 Valiant with their personal things and park it in the garage of Christina

Petsas. They boarded an airplane out of Chicago for Greece about a week before Christmas.

It was the first time Vasilis visited Greece in five years. It was the first time ever for Kay to visit Greece and meet Vasilis' family. There is not much remembered about the flight, except it was full of excitement and anticipation and the awareness that God is faithful in keeping His promises and directing the steps of those who are faithful. It was a great homecoming. Vasilis had the opportunity to share with the church in Athens and then he and Kay spent precious time with the family. The family was both excited and well pleased to meet Kay. They were deeply impressed with her and she captured their hearts. What a joy and what refreshing days enjoying the fellowship and the delicious meals with the family.

After their Christmas visit to Greece, Vasilis and Kay returned to Chicago, entered their 1965 Valiant, which was parked at the house of Christina, and headed for Wilmore, Kentucky. On the way there Vasilis was a little apprehensive about school, how they were going to pay the bills, and how they could make a living. He verbalized his concerns to Kay and then raised the question, "What would we do if we get there and we do not get any invitations for meetings? As you know there are not many people who know us there." Instead of responding to his question, Kay simply began to sing a stanza from the hymn, "God will take care of you". Then she turned the radio on that was set on a Christian radio station and guess what? The same song came over the airwaves! The Lord knows how to convict and humble a preacher. God used the experience to help Vasilis focus his trust on Him, and that He had already gone before him and had made the preparations. It is not how many people we know, but how well we know God and trust in Him. Paul was right when he said to the Philippians, "My God shall supply all your needs."

159

Vasilis and Kay got busy in pursuing the purpose for which they went and God began to honor their faith by fulfilling His promises. They began to receive invitations for ministering through the preached word, the first one coming from the church in Richmond, Kentucky, where Jay Hartman was the pastor. He also preached at the First Church of God in Winchester, Kentucky, which he would pastor 28 years later. But God had other surprises in providing for their needs. The school informed Vasilis that an anonymous person began to deposit in the school for Vasilis' account $250.00 per month. The irony of this is that a year later, a month or so before they decided to leave school, the check stopped coming and no one knew they were leaving. The surprise did not stop there. The school had given Vasilis a partial scholarship and after three months they called him in and offered him a full conditional scholarship. The condition was that after his studies he must agree that he would return to Greece. He then asked the question, "What if God does not want me to return to Greece?" He rejected the scholarship because he wanted to be free to do whatever God had for him and wherever God wanted to lead him.

Vasilis and Kay remember their days in Asbury with great amusement and a smile on their face. They recall the faithfulness of God, the providential angels of God, the humorous things that took place and the obstacles and the challenges they faced. Memories all bring a smile with a sense of gratitude. When people asked them about their grocery budget, Vasilis answered that they had worked out a good menu. They had peas and potatoes one day and the next day they had potatoes and peas! Their biggest and most enjoyable treat was, when they were able, to go to Jerry's restaurant in Lexington and order a piece of strawberry pie.

It was amazing how God would open doors for ministry for the weekends and during vacations from West Virginia to Illinois, Ohio and other places. During the summer of 1968 they decided to take two young sisters from the Hope Hill Children's Home and keep them for a week. They were orphans and they had a brother also who was in the home named Bombo. Whether that was his real name or a nickname, they were not sure. It was at that time that they received an invitation to preach for the first weekend of August at the Allison's Gap Church of God in Saltville, Virginia. Kay felt uneasy taking the girls with them.

On Saturday, August 3, 1968, about noon, they left Wilmore, stopped by Hope Hill Children's Home, dropped the girls off and they continued their journey to Saltville, Virginia, on route 460 east. It was late afternoon when they crossed into Lebanon, Virginia. A brief shower came and as Vasilis was driving down the hill, the car began sliding, the wheels locked, he lost control, hit a fence pole, then a tree and ended up in the middle of a cow pasture. The car was all messed up, the doors would not open and smoke was coming out of the engine. Both of them were in a daze, Vasilis bleeding from his head, and Kay was hurting in the abdomen. Since the doors would not open, he sat there without any effort to help Kay or try to get out of the car. After a few moments in silence, Kay looked at Vasilis and said, "Don't just sit there. Do something." To which he replied, "What do you want me to do?" Her response, "At least you can pray." He did pray, but he does not recall one word of what he said. After prayer as he tried again to open the door, the door did open and both of them were able to get out of the car.

They were sitting there in the middle of the cow pasture without a living, breathing thing in sight, and it was approaching sunset. They were both hurting but there was no way to get help. They managed to get closer to the road in case a car passed by while a host of questions were racing through their mind. "Why did this happen?" "What about the preaching appointment the next day?" "What about school?" The car was totaled, they would be without transportation, and they were not sure how bad they were hurt. The only comfort at the moment appeared to be that "God works in all things together for good to those who love Him" (Rom. 8:28- *paraphrase mine).*

No one recalls how much time elapsed, but in the distance they saw a yellow Volkswagen coming and Vasilis flagged it down. It did stop and it was loaded with four fishermen. They were very kind and they offered to take them to the Lebanon Hospital. The only thing Vasilis took from the car was a handkerchief in which he had tied some half dollar silver coins, enough for gas to get back to Wilmore. They squeezed Vasilis and Kay in the car and took them to the hospital. As they were dropping them off, Vasilis opened his handkerchief to pay them, but they were kind and felt sorry for them and did not take anything. Who would have the heart to take money from a fellow who was all beaten up, his thoughts were not very clear, his wife was going to be admitted to the hospital and the only thing he had was a few silver half-dollar coins?

They were rushed into the emergency room. Vasilis received some stitches and band aids on his head and face and was released, but Kay was admitted from fear that she might have some internal injuries. They had no way to communicate with the church and they were at a loss to know what to do. It was at that time that Vasilis remembered that his friend Neville Mozingo was pastoring in the neighboring town from Saltville, Marion. He called him and he came and helped Vasilis make some arrangements for the car and took him to the house of John and Ted Elmore in Saltville while Kay remained in the hospital. They were more than kind, hospitable and encouraging.

When Sunday morning came, Vasilis was sore, black and blue eyes, band aids on his head and face and hardly could move. Vasilis recalls the expressions of the people that Sunday morning as they walked into the sanctuary and saw him sitting on the platform with black and blue eyes and band aids all over his face. They did not know anything about the accident, so they were free to draw their own conclusions. The sight of Vasilis that morning did not appear that he belonged at the pulpit.

The service was a moving experience and with good response. The leadership decided on the spot that due to the circumstances the services would be extended through Wednesday and change it to a revival meeting. After the service and after lunch some men took Vasilis to see Kay and return back in time for the evening service. On Monday Kay was released from the hospital. The car was totaled and since there was no collision insurance, it was a complete loss. He does not recall if he got anything out of the car. After the meeting they returned to Lexington, flying out of Tri-City Airport and on their way to Wilmore. Vasilis had to finish a Greek class he was taking that summer before he could do anything else.

Why do bad things happen to good people? Did God cause the accident? Certainly not! Did God use the accident to direct their life and accomplish His purpose and will? He certainly did! It could be because Greeks have the name of being hardheaded that it was the only way for the Lord to have Vasilis' full attention. You see, Vasilis was pulled in two different directions while in Asbury. On the one side he was so enamored with academia that he could have become a professional student. On the other hand, there was a fire or a burden within him for evangelism and missions, which became more intense as he was sitting under the teaching of Dr. Robert Coleman and Dr. Dennis Kinlaw. The accident helped Vasilis to put things into perspective and without the accident it is doubtful that he would have ever accepted the pastorate in Saltville, VA. It was that experience that had such drastic and lasting effects in the direction of their life and ministry. It was in times such as these that the words of Joseph came alive and made sense, "Ye thought evil against me; but God meant it for good," (Gen. 50:20 KJV).

The Saltville Church extended them a call to become its pastors and after the summer class had finished by the first of September, they were moved to Saltville.   The Asbury experience, even though short, served them well and intensified their determination to be flames for God and His Kingdom. As Dr. Robert Coleman used to say to his class on evangelism concerning men who gave their all and made an impact in the kingdom, "Boys, flames are bright, but they do not last long." Vasilis just wanted to keep the flame burning!

THE MOUNTAIN EXPERIENCE
AND THE MISSIONAL FOCUS

**Vasilis, Kay with Jonathan and the congregation
1971 or 1972**

"Whoever serves me must follow me; and where I am, my servants also will be. My Father will honor the one who serves me"

John 12:26 (NIV).

It was the first weekend of September in 1968 when three men from the Saltville congregation pulled up at the duplex apartment in Wilmore with a U-Haul. They do not recall all the men with the exception of John Henry Elmore, who turned out to become one of their best friends. While the other men were loading the truck, John Henry was gathering tomatoes from some tomato vines that Vasilis had planted in the flowerbed on the side of the apartment. His excuse was when the men asked him to help, "There was no need for those tomatoes to go to waste!"

Saltville, even though it was a mountainous area, proved to be a fertile station for their life and ministry. It served as an incubator to nurture their burning desire for evangelism and missions. There was a release of the Spirit of God upon them and the church that it was noticeable and both they and the church placed their focus on missions and evangelism.

Vasilis' life and ministry at Saltville, Virginia, was both exciting and rewarding in more than one way. One of the most significant events that took place in 1972 was taking the oath to become a citizen of the United States in Abingdon, Virginia. He did so with pride, eagerness and loyalty. He had studied the history and the constitution of the U.S.A. as well as its branches of government. He was both inspired and excited considering the way his world-view was shaped by his past experiences.

The day arrived when he and seven others from different countries stood before the judge in a citizenship ceremony in Abingdon, Virginia. There was music, pledging allegiance to the flag, and then a local pastor offered a prayer of dedication. Vasilis' eyes were misty, his heart was leaping with joy, having the privilege and the responsibility to participate in the American dream. He says, "I felt like I was reborn. Who am I, a boy who had grown up in war and poverty, and whose life was full of uncertainty, to be given the privilege of freedom and the opportunity and honor to serve?"

It was in this lovely place that Vasilis and Kay's two boys were born, Jonathan and David, and where they learned to do cartwheels in the front of a full sanctuary while their mother was playing the piano. In retrospect, Vasilis states their ministry could not have taken the shape it did and they could not have walked in the many doors of God-given opportunity without the sacrifice, faithfulness and the constant support of his wife, Kay. She raised the two boys single-handedly while pursuing studies and being involved in ministry.

Kay, Jonathan and Vasilis 1972

The Saltville experience was very unique in ministry and very eventful with unbelievable surprises. It was the only place where at times people would call or knock at the door of the parsonage with the words, "I want to get saved." There was a weekly radio program, "The Deeper Life', broadcast and multiple doors of opportunity. It was during that time that God placed some people in the life of Vasilis that would play a significant role in the future: Mayo McIntyre, Maurice Berquist, Homer and Vivian Gentry, John Henry and Ted Elmore, Gene and Shirley Little, Janet Atkins Stevenson, and others.

It was in the midst of the most exciting and rewarding time of ministry in that wonderful place with such a loving people, an opportunity knocked at their door that presented itself very attractive to Vasilis. Both Nick Zazanis, former missionary to Greece, and the Missionary Board corresponded with them about the possibility of

Mayo McIntyre with Vasilis 1976

returning to Greece as missionaries to lead the church there and assist with the possibility of establishing a Mediterranean Bible College that had been proposed. There was much excitement and anticipation. There was an exchange of correspondence and meetings. What was envisioned was fitting within the scope and the vision of Vasilis' involvement in the church, not only in Greece but also in Europe. Everything appeared to be ready to go.

When Vasilis was about to make the final decision and say, "Yes", a fear gripped his heart that he could not say yes. As he stated later, "Every moment that I was ready to make the final decision, the green light within me would turn red and everything was brought to a stop." His hesitation was intensified later when the Missionary Board, being influenced by the church in Beirut, Lebanon, decided to place the college there. Vasilis thought his involvement with the college could provide more outlets for ministry and an opportunity to influence young people. But nevertheless, he was willing to comply with God's will and go to Greece. But every time the call would come for a response, the green light would turn red and that convinced Vasilis it was not the will of God for them to go, no matter how much they wanted to do it. They declined the invitation on the basis of that experience.

Shortly after Vasilis had rejected the invitation to return to Greece, he had a very unusual experience. Quite often early in the morning, he would meet with men who worked on shift and could not attend church regularly and spend some time with them in prayer and Bible study. One morning in August 1973 as the men left, he went to the altar of the church to spend some time in prayer. As he was praying the impression came upon him that he should go to Africa. He did not know what to think about such a thought and soon dismissed it as a flare up of his childhood dreams about Africa. He thought he did not have any connections with the church of Africa, except that the church was supporting the missionaries Edna Thimes and Stanley Hoffman, and possibly one more missionary, and they had supported some other projects. Even though he dismissed the thought, from time to time it would reenter his mind.

It was a month later at the same place while in prayer that the same thought invaded his mind, "You will go to Africa." This time he became a little more preoccupied with the thought and raised the question, "Could it be from the Lord?" He decided to put it to the test in a very unorthodox way. He took $5.00 and he went straight to the bank and opened a savings account with the name, "Mission 74, A Faith Mission", and he said, "Lord, if this is from you, you will have

169

to confirm it in a significant way." The next day he decided to share with his church secretary about the experience that he had and her immediate response was, "I believe it is from the Lord, here is $10.00 to put into that account!" A couple days later he went to Bristol and he visited Glen More's Clothing Store. One of the salesmen was a good friend of Vasilis, a devout Christian and quite often they engaged in theological discussion and prayer. Vasilis shared his unusual experience with him and his immediate response was as Ed began crying, "I believe this is from the Lord, and I want to have a part in it. Here is $20.00, put it in that account."

All these responses and others were good and positive, but they were not the kind of confirmation he was looking for. There was no doubt there was excitement in Vasilis and his anticipation was growing but he was wondering, how would he really know what this was all about? It was about two or three weeks later that he had the surprise of his life. He received a letter from Eliazer Mdobi, Secretary of the Church of God in Tanzania, East Africa, inviting him to be the speaker for their national convention in 1974. Wow! Soon afterwards there was a letter from Stanley Hoffman, missionary to Tanzania, stating that in the late summer in 1974 the church for which Vasilis' church had sent the money to be built would be ready and he wondered if Vasilis could come and preach the dedication. It was not much later when Vasilis received another letter from Bynum Makokha, Secretary of the Church of God in Kenya, inviting Vasilis to be the speaker for their leadership conference and for their national convention which would follow the conference.

What a confirmation and what a surprise! What made things more interesting was the way all these events were scheduled. The dedication of the church was at the end of July, the Tanzanian conventions in the first part of August and the Kenyan leadership conference and convention close to the middle of August. God even works out the details in the scheduling! But that is not all, there was correspondence in October from the Santanocitos in Rome, Italy and the LaFonts in Beirut, Lebanon, which served as confirmation and which became part of the adventure of faith. There was no doubt that this endeavor was ordained by the Lord.

In 1974 Africa was experiencing a severe drought and the church and the orphanage in Beirut, Lebanon, were going through difficult times. Vasilis thought because of his forthcoming visit to those places, people might be willing to help, so he began to promote a request for the help of the church in Tanzania, Kenya and the orphanage in Beirut. But he was not prepared for what followed. The Saltville Progress picked up the story and it ran like a wild fire. Gifts began to come from everywhere, Baptists, Methodists, Nazarenes, the Christian Church, and the Episcopalians and from people in the community and from the area churches of God. It became bigger than anyone had envisioned. So Vasilis very quickly appointed a committee of five to handle the gifts and requests and to properly document and receipt them properly. It was strictly for the relief of the churches in Tanzania and Kenya and the orphanage in Beirut.

The plans for Mission 74 – A Faith Mission – were finalized. Vasilis took forty days leave of absence from the church without pay, he borrowed some money for family and personal expenses with the plans that on the 22nd of July, Kay and the two boys would accompany him to Rome, and from there they would catch a plane to Athens and stay with Vasilis' family while he would continue on to Africa. Upon completion of his trip, he would stop by Greece, spend a week with the family and then all together they would return home. But sometimes things do not always work the way we plan them.

THE TRIP TO AFRICA

On July 20, 1974, all was ready to go, details in place and with full anticipation to explore what God had planned ahead. But early in the morning of July 21st, the news broke out that Turkey had invaded Cyprus and that both Turkey and Greece were in a state of war with the airports being closed and the Greek army had started to recall all those who had been discharged. Vasilis and Kay found themselves with a dilemma, but immediately their decision was made that Vasilis should proceed with the planned missions trip, and Kay and the boys should remain back and evaluate the situation. If things changed, then they would proceed with their plans and inform Vasilis accordingly. But things did not work out, Kay and the boys never made it to Greece and she never was able to communicate with Vasilis.

Vasilis' trip did not go on without any change and obstacles either. On his first stop in Rome, he found a mechanics' strike in the airport that delayed him for three days. Beirut was his next stop on the missions trip, but it was closed due to the Greece-Turkey situation. Vasilis was troubled by the second change because he had some supplies for the missionaries there and some money for the orphanage. But God always has a plan and He makes provision ahead of time. While at the church in Ostia, Italy, he met a sister who was working for the orphanage in Beirut. She was on vacation in Switzerland, and she was going to be able to enter Lebanon by boat from Egypt. That solved Vasilis' problem. He sent with her what he had for the missionaries and the orphanage.

Due to the changes he had to spend a full day in Cairo before he could continue on to Tanzania. Wanting to meet some brothers in Egypt whose address was in his possession, he decided to take a taxi and go to locate them. But upon arrival in their place, he was informed they had traveled to Alexandria. The taxi driver saw the disappointment on his face and offered to take Vasilis to some important place in Cairo without any extra charge. They spent at least two hours together and in the process the driver found out all about Vasilis' trip and its purpose. But Vasilis was not prepared for the response of the driver upon returning to the airport, and when Vasilis asked him, "What do I owe you?" the driver responded, "Look, I know that you are going to a missions trip in Tanzania and Kenya. If you do not have the money, you can wait till you get back to America and then you can send it to me!" Wow! What was this kind of words from a stranger? But Vasilis paid the fare, which was not much and spent the rest of the time in the airport, drinking Egyptian tea with a postman, learning about Egypt and sharing his faith in Christ. The postman was so moved that when Vasilis started to leave, he gave him some Egyptian collection stamps.

As he boarded the airplane in Cairo for Nairobi, Kenya, and then on to Arusia, Tanzania, his heart was filled with the excitement of a child and he was imagining all the things that he was going to see and experience. The Hoffmans picked him up at the airport and they arrived safely at the Kaiti Mission Station. As he spent the first night of his visit there, he did not sleep much that night. Every time he heard a noise he would get up and go and look outside the window, expecting to see a tiger, a lion or a leopard. But every time he looked, he was disappointed; the only thing he saw was bushes moving by blowing in the wind.

He visited the Wuabulu Mission Station where Bob and Janet Edwards were serving, the future Babbati Mission Station and on to Mirambo Station where Roy and Magdalene Hoops were serving. The most moving experience was when he visited the Massai tribe with Rufus and the dedication of the new church for which the Saltville church had sent the money. What deeply impressed him were not just the faithfulness of the missionaries but the power and the impact of the gospel upon the lives of the people as well as the joy and the transformed lives that were displayed. Vasilis was like a little child who suddenly was thrown in the arena of his heart's desire, full of wonder, excitement and amazement.

THE TANZANIA CONVENTION

When the first night for the convention arrived, Vasilis was surprised to see their missionary guests from Kenya such as Edna Thimes, Mr. and Mrs. Doug Welch, Mr. and Mrs. Aaron Kerr and others. Eliazer Mdobi, the Secretary of the Church, was assigned to be Vasilis' interpreter. What a Christian gentleman! What a sweet and servant-like spirit! He was so eager to do his best so that the message of the word should be communicated correctly, he would spend about thirty minutes with Vasilis before each service in prayer and going over the main points of the message. Vasilis states he has had several people interpret for him, but none with the spirit and sensitiveness of Eliazer.

As the service commenced an excitement filled the air with expectation. The music was outstanding and the rhythm could cause even the mute to sing. The message was on the Holy Spirit and His work in the life of the believer. It was a great service with some response, but both Vasilis, some of the missionaries, and some of the local leaders of the church felt there appeared to be a hindering spirit in the service. After the service, the Hoffmans had invited all the missionaries present to their house located in the missions compound. All came with the exception of one couple. It was an enjoyable time of fellowship, but the conversation was centered around the message on the Holy Spirit with a lot of questions. It was past 11:00 p.m. when Stanley Hoffman asked Roy Hoops to lead in prayer so everyone could go to their lodging place.

Roy had not said five words in his prayer when he suddenly stopped and said, "Stan, I want you to forgive me, I have been harboring some hard feelings toward you!" What followed afterwards can only be described as a moving of the Holy Spirit. There was confession after confession. There were tears and there was a settling of the sweet presence of the Holy Spirit with great rejoicing. It was past midnight when finally the fellowship was dismissed, but a spark had been ignited by the Holy Spirit in the hearts of those who were present. Vasilis recalls the words of Edna Thimes saying,"I wish that so and so could be here (names withheld)."

The next morning the first thing on the agenda was the ministers' meeting. As the meeting began, it was evident the special guest that morning was the Holy Spirit. What happened the night before was happening now among the ministers. There was confessions,

Vasilis is presented with a spear from the leaders of the church there.

tears and asking for forgiveness. Joy and praise filled the place. The remaining part of the convention was saturated with the presence and the power of the Holy Spirit.

There were many events in which Vasilis participated. He traveled with Sister Hoffman to witness a birth in the bush. He even participated in marriages, African style and the ritual of gift presentation. He visited with the Massai warriors. There was a custom in that part of the country at that time that when a child was born it would be given the name of something special that was happening during that time. Well, the only thing named after Vasilis is now a goat had a little kid and they called it "Billy"!

Vasilis trying to lead a goat

THE KENYA ADVENTURE

Upon arriving in Kenya, Vasilis was graciously hosted by the Kerns, the Welches, the Makokhas, Edna Thimes and Nasser and Merilyn Farag. The first Sunday he preached in three churches in Nairobi with some of the most unusual experiences. In the last service of the day a congregation of about 750 waited almost two hours for Vasilis to arrive. He preached for fifteen minutes, and then they spent about 45 minutes praying with those who had responded. The wonderful thing about the experience was that nothing was controlled by the clock. Bynum Makokha took Vasilis to every district to meet with the pastors. Nasser Farah exposed him to new approaches to ministry at Kisi. Aaron Kern gave him a tour of the Nairobi park and Edna Thimes took him to the Massai Country. After all these adventures and experiences which constitute a book in themselves, it was time for the big events, the leadership conference and the convention.

A typical Masai family

The leadership conference was held in the cathedral, a large building that was built years before. Vasilis was told they had 1,500 delegates. The spirit and the response were great. People responded freely and they prayed earnestly, expecting God to honor their prayers. Vasilis recalls on one occasion as people responded, service after service by the dozens, he was invited to pray with a lady who appeared to be under great stress and very emotional. They explained to him the lady could not have

177

any children and she felt she was a reproach to her husband and family. She wanted Vasilis to pray that the Lord will give her a child. Vasilis' heart stopped for a second, he had never prayed before for anything like that. But is there anything too big for God? Vasilis prayed as all the brethren around him joined in. They claimed the promises of God and asked that God would glorify His name. Vasilis returned home and soon forgot about the situation. A year or so later one of the missionaries communicated with him (possibly Edna Thimes) and told him the lady did have a child!

After the conference, the convention was moved outdoors because of the great number of people that were attending. It was both an interesting and moving experience for Vasilis. He was told there could be from 10,000 to 15,000 people in attendance, but Vasilis thought probably something like 5,000 or 7,000; no one knew for sure. One thing was fully evident, the presence of the Holy Spirit and the power of God's word as well as the hunger of the people. Vasilis was amazed at the transforming power of God's word in the life of people as story after story was shared with him. What an experience! What an exposure! What an inspiration! God never makes mistakes when we allow him to direct our steps. Does not the scripture say to acknowledge Him in all our ways and He will direct our steps?

As the 38-day missionary journey was coming to a close, he had not heard anything from the family. He made some effort to get in touch with the American Embassy and learn something about the Greece-Turkey situation over Cyprus. It was only then that Bynum Makokha informed him about a telegram that had come from his wife and he had lost it. He was not aware of what message it said! The American Embassy advised Vasilis not to travel to Greece. Not only because the situation was tense and serious, but also Vasilis was facing the possibility of being drafted into the Greek army in spite of the fact that he was an American citizen. (In Greece, once a Greek always a Greek. They never disclaim you.)

The plans were changed and Vasilis bypassed Greece and flew to Brussels instead and from there to the United States. It might be appropriate to finish the story of the journey with something humorous and yet true. On the flight from Nairobi to Brussels, Vasilis sat in the airplane between a Muslim businessman on his left and a young Christian lady who was working for some Para church organization on his right. She was going to London. As the plane was crossing over the Sahara Desert, it hit a couple air pockets and it dropped considerably which left people both speechless and with fear. In fact the color in most of the people's faces had changed. Vasilis loves adventure and things like this present a challenge for him. He never exchanged a word with the businessman on his left. His body language showed that he did not want to be bothered. But Vasilis turned to the young lady on his right with this question, "Are you afraid?" The response was quick and to the point, "Sure, I am." Then Vasilis proceeded to give reassurance by saying,"There is no need to be afraid, this plane is not going to go down!" The young lady with a puzzled look and bewilderment on her face said, "How do you know that this plane is not going to go down?" "Well," responded Vasilis, "It is something like this. I believe that God sent me to Africa for 38 days and I did what I felt to be His will and now I am on my way home to see my wife and my two boys. I do not believe that God would take me to Africa and then on my way home He would drop me over the Sahara Desert! Besides there is a scripture which says, 'The Lord shall preserve your going out and your coming in from this time forth, and even forevermore" (Psalm 121:8). This is a promise that God would be with us when we go out and when we come back in!" It was not clear whether the young lady was satisfied or convinced with Vasilis' response of reassurance, but one thing is absolutely clear and that is that the airplane did not go down!

BACK ON THE MOUNTAINOUS EXPERIENCE

Saltville Virginia is a humble place with its simple and loving people. It was in the midst of an explosive ministry in Saltville, that God placed certain people in Vasilis' path. People who not only made great contribution to his ministry, but also proved to be longlasting friends. Mayo McIntyre was a lady preacher who at one time had pastored the church in Saltville. She was a dynamic preacher, a prayer warrior who could move heaven and an excellent Sunday School teacher. Her faith and commitment to the truth were unshakable. Her counsel and support proved invaluable. What a spiritaul dynamite!

It was in this place that Vasilis got acquainted with Maurice Berquist. He was married to Bernice McIntyre, Mayo's daughter. They were frequent visitors to Saltville and the church. At the beginning Vasilis did not know how to react to Berquist because of his humor, but the more he came to know him, the more he appreciated his genuis and his love for the Lord and His Church. It was Maurice who taught Vasilis how to conduct surveys for witnessing, the proper use of the four spiritual laws, and how to organize tours with a mission to the Bible lands.

The two became good friends, getting involved in deep theological discussions and sharing in several settings and platforms through the years. He was unique either way you could measure him and he always expressed himself in unique ways. On one occasion he was visiting Saltville and went to church service on Wednesday evening. Vasilis was conducting a Bible study on the First Epistle of John. The attendance was great, the spirit warm and the Bible study illuminating with truth to which the people responded well with comments. At the conclusion.Vasilis had prayer and dismissed the service. The people began to fellowship as they were exiting the building. Vasilis noticed that Maurice had not moved from his pew. He was sitting there with his arms crossed and appeared to be in deep thought. When Vasilis approached him and extended his hand to shake hands with him, he refused! He was upset because Vasilis had not given an altar call. He said, "Why? Why did you not give an altar call after such a moving message? It was evident that the Spirit was present and at work." Vasilis responded, "Maurice, this is Wednesday evening. We just have our people here, I did not sense the need for an altar call." But he fired back without hesitation, "It does not make any difference, you should have given an altar call." He was unique. Quite often he would say to Vasilis, "Bernice wants me to have you down in the Daytona church, because she says, 'nobody can say things the way you do.'" He was present when Vasilis preached his mother-in-law's funeral and that of Dr. William Allison. After the Allison funeral, he and another person requested to ride with Vasilis to the cemetery. On the way to the cemetery he turned to the other person in the car and said, "Vasilis makes the funeral service so interesting and so exciting that it makes you to want to die right away and go to heaven!"

There were some other significant encounters with individuals who God had placed on Vasilis' path. One Sunday morning while the service was in progress and the sanctuary was practically full, a tall couple with a touch of silver in their hair and with a sweet young boy walked into the sanctuary. Being no space anywhere else, they were ushered and sat on the second pew from the front. They were Homer, Vivian and Jimmy Gentry from Abingdon, Virginia, whose roots were in Todd, North Carolina. Vivian was the daugthter of Ed Blackburn, one of the most graceful, lovng and humble elderly holiness preachers, who had both a church and a holiness camp meeting at Todd, North Carolin. They had gone to Saltville "to check both the church and the preacher out because they had heard so much about them." What a people! What an influence on Vasilis and what a great relationship with the whole family through the years! Brother Blackburn had Vasilis several times as speaker in the holiness camp meeting and Vasilis always considered it as a highlight of his ministry to be in that place and share with Brother Ed, his wife and his family; Homer and Vivian, Ben and Betty, Lillian and Bower as well as their extended family.

Saltville was not far from Abingdon, Chilhowie and Marion, Virginia. Vasilis' radio program, "The Deeper Life Broadcast", which had a reach of about seventy or one hundred miles with his distinct accent gave him an easy recognition. In Chilhowie, there was a couple with the name Eugene and Shirley Little, with their three children Tom, Karla and Jeff. Gene was a businessman who had been saved recently, was on fire for the Lord and he was searching for God's direction for his life. Divine providence brought Vasilis and Gene together. There was a bond that developed between them that has been going on for almost 40 years. It was not long afterwards that Gene felt his call to the ministry. He went to school and then founded the Glade Spring Church of God. He got involved in radio ministry and became a very effective pastor with the heart of both a shepherd and an evangelist. In reflecting on his relationship with Gene, Vasilis states, "I do not know if and in what ways I have been helpful to Gene, but certainly he has been an angel of the Lord in my journey of faith and in many times and in many ways has refreshed my soul!"

Quite often when Vasilis reflects on the people that God had placed on his path throughout the years, he would say, "Some day, I would like to write a book entitled, Angels On My Journey, reflecting on the graciousness of God and the sensitivity of certain people to be obedient as they were prompted by the Holy Spirit."

John Henry and Ted Elmore, together with John's mother, Sister Carrie Elmore, were another people the Lord had brought into Vasilis' life and minsitry who became like family. The Elmores served as Vasilis and Kay's hosts when they first visited the church. Since then they have been adopted as

182

members of the family and they have been treated that way since 1968. Their hospitality, support, faithfulness and their spiritual growth have greatly contributed to Vasilis' life and ministry. Their home has been Vasilis' home, their car always at his disposal when in need. Their love has been unconditional and their friendship rewarding in any way you measure it.

It would be almost impossible to make references to the many lives that might have been touched by Vasilis' life and ministry. It would be equally impossible to name the many people whose hearts were touched by God and who were placed by God in his journey of faith in order to enhance both his life and ministry. Most of the things that God does in our life and most of the blessings that He sends into our life, come through people who are sensitive to His voice and who are motivated by His love.

In 1969, during the tax season, Vasilis was introduced to Janet Atkins, now Stevenson, a tax lady from Marion, Virginia. After she had prepared Vasilis' taxes, she refused to receive payment with these words, "This is my ministry, and I am blessed in doing it." For more than forty years she has executed this ministry for Kay and Vasilis, even when they were overseas. Not only this, but her support and that of her husband for Vasilis and Kay's ministry could not be put into words and a thousand "Thank you's could not come even close to capture their gratitude; nor can one measure the encouragement and support that they provided for their ministry.

Upon reflection, they are always amazed that in every location God directed their life and ministry and under every circumstance that confronted their life and ministry, God always and without exception, had placed some choice people in their journey who indeed were the angels of God.

In reading Paul's Epistle to Philemon, you get the impression that Paul had such people placed before him no matter where he went, who refreshed his soul and who were koinonoi or partakers of his Gospel ministry. Besides, does not Jesus say that he who forsakes mother, father, brother and sister for His sake, not only he would have eternal life, but also he would receive hundredfold of the family he forsook for the Kingdom's sake?(Matt. 19:29 *paraphrase mine).*

MISSIONS RUMBLINGS AND THE CALL

Kay, Jonathan, David and Vasilis

"Therefore go and make disciples of all nations, baptizing them in the name of the Father and of the Son and of the Holy Spirit, and teaching them to obey everything I have commanded you. And surely I am with you always, to the end of the age"

(Mathew 28:19-20 NIV).

Vasilis' missionary journey to Africa was not just a missions trip but a life-transforming experience. It rekindled his previous passion for missions, it changed both his attitude and outlook and made a lasting impact upon his life. He always has said he was not sure how much good he did in Africa and if he had any impact on the church there, but he was absolutely certain that the trip made a difference in his life and had an impact in the outlook of his ministry. He spoke about our responsibility of sharing the Gospel with the peoples of the world and our response to the poor people of the world with passion and conviction as a Biblical mandate for the church.

His two boys listened to story after story at the dinner table, especially when they were reluctant to eat their food. The words always would come from their father, "There are a lot of children in Africa that they would have liked to have what you have to eat!" That was repeated around the table several times in the course of two or three months. So much, that one day, the oldest son, Jonathan, about five years old at the time, looked at his dad and said, "Dad, I have an idea. Let's sell all we have and give the money to those poor children in Africa, so we would not have to listen to the same story every time we sit at the table to have dinner!" He did not know at that time that he spoke prophetically, because children like those were going to be his playmates and schoolmates later.

There was almost nothing Vasilis did not like or enjoy in the ministry. His level of excitement, commitment and anticipation continued with a passion in his soul which at times made him restless and frustrated because others did not share his level of passion and anticipation. All his involvement and all the demands upon his life did not quite bring the level of satisfaction and contentment that he sought in ministry. There were a lot of happenings in his life and ministry, but something from within was calling for another step of faith and another level of commitment. There were calls for new pastorates but that did not appeal to him. His involvement in the state and national levels of ministry did not quench the quest of his vision for the world, what the New Testament calls, "The regions beyond".

It was during that time the Missionary Board of the Church of God contacted Vasilis to see if he would be willing and available to serve as missionary in Argentina, South America. It is hard to tell what Vasilis' initial reaction was to the invitation, because his heart was captivated by Africa. But he was willing to explore God's will and do whatever that will require.

In his first meeting with the representative of the Missionary Board who Vasilis does not want to identify, he made known his interest toward Africa, to which the Missionary Board representative said, "I do not know much about you, except that you are a good preacher. I do not think Africa would be a good match for you." While the conversation continued in different stages, it became clear to both Vasilis and Kay that God was calling them to Argentina, and what followed afterwards did not cause any doubts. It was then that Vasilis remembered that God was at work before he knew anything about Argentina. Now he understood why he was impressed to take Spanish while he was in college. In January 1976 they gave their response to the Missionary Board, "Yes".

In February 1976, Gulf Coast Bible College had invited Vasilis and Kay to attend the Minister's Refresher Institute in Houston, Texas. They had a presentation for them. The alumni association had chosen him to receive the "Max R. Gaulke Award in Missions, Education and Evangelism". The following month they tendered their resignation to the church, effective June 9, 1976. The resignation sent shock waves both across the church and the community. So Vasilis, Kay and the two boys began their preparation for the journey of faith with the first stop in San Jose, Costa Rica, for language school.

The exodus from the First Church of God, the town of Saltville, and even Southwest Virginia, was very emotional and demonstrative of how much they were loved by the people and of how much they loved the people. It will be difficult for words to capture the emotional uproar of the last couple or three months. They sold or gave away almost everything. The one exception came when Kay decided to store their piano with one of the families of the church. At the last minute, Kay said, "I do not know when I will come back or if I will ever come back, it will be better if we sold the piano." And she did.

Their farewell was not just a farewell of the church but of the whole town and even Southwest Virginia. The church planned a meal and reserved the high school cafeteria. Then they planned a service after the meal and reserved the high school auditorium. They invited Vasilis and Kay's friends, the Sing Time Quartet to do the singing, Brice Casey to do the preaching. All the town ministers were present and a great number from the Church of God across the state. The mayor, town officials, business people and lay people were present. Bill Henderson, owner and director of the only funeral home in town pulled Vasilis to the side and whispered in his ear, "As far as I am concerned the inspiration of our town is leaving!" Then he made Vasilis promise that he would return to conduct his funeral no matter where he was or what the cost. Little did he know that he was going to die at 57 before Vasilis left the country.

The farewell was a warm, emotional celebration that was closing a special chapter of their journey of faith in the hills of Southwest Virginia. They were ready to begin another whose happenings were yet to be discovered. The church presented the family with four tickets for a trip to Greece to visit with the family before they left for South America. People showered them with gifts, best wishes, letters and prayers. What a church! What a place! What a people! What an expression of love! Who could ever think that God would take a poor boy out of the hills of Southern Greece and transplant him in the hills of Southwest Virginia as a vibrant witness of the Gospel of Jesus Christ? The greatest luxury of life, in spite of its events and circumstances, is to live in the center of God's will. That is life's greatest satisfaction.

On June 9, 1976, the family traveled to Anderson, Indiana to participate in the International Convention of the Church of God, where they were commissioned as missionaries to Argentina, together with others who were going in different places around the world. After the convention, Vasilis and the family traveled to Greece to spend almost three weeks with his family. It was the last time for Vasilis to see his mother, who upon greeting him in his departure said to him prophetically, "I will not see you again in this world", and then she threw her arms around his neck and she would not let it go.

The last day with the family was July 14. It was an evening that brought the whole family together and where a lot of emotions were unleashed. They celebrated David's birthday in the backyard of the house. His birthday actually was on the 15th but since they were going to be traveling, they celebrated it early. What a family! What a love! What a sacrifice and support for Vasilis and Kay's ministry! Vasilis always said that if there was any usefulness of his ministry in the Kingdom and for the Kingdom of God it was due to the prayers of his mother. Even though he did not see her face anymore, her presence and her prayers followed him around the world and she remained alive in his memory with her spirit of love and sacrifice.

DIVINE INTERRUPTIONS AND DETOURS

Vasilis and his family committed themselves for the country of Argentina for a five-fold purpose: a. Help to facilitate the transition of the church from the German language into Spanish; b. Teach at the Instituto Biblico; c. Work in leadership development; d. Assist in the planting of new churches; and e. Conduct evangelistic meetings throughout the country and maintain contact with Uruguay and Chile. But they were not aware that God had some other short plans and assignments before it was the right time for Argentina.

The first stop in the missionary journey was language school from August to May in San Jose, Costa Rica. Since Vasilis had two years Spanish in college, he underestimated the demands of the language, he decided to enroll in the In Service Program of Fuller Seminary and take some courses in Anthropology, Missions and Church Growth. It proved to be a challenge, but it provided a clear understanding in the difference of cultures and group dynamics. The language school experience, the involvement in the life of the church in Costa Rica, and their relationship with both resident and student missionaries, the Nachtigall's and the Zoretic's, not only provided some social outlet but also an understanding of the practical life of a missionary in a different culture.

In the late winter and early spring of 1977, El Salvador had gone through a political turmoil, and the church was challenged from every direction. It was decided that Paul Zoretic and Vasilis would take their spring vacation from language school and together with the Nachtigalls, travel to El Salvador to encourage the church in the capitol city, San Salvador. The situation was very tense. The massacre that had taken place in the capital just a few months before and the disappearance of people from time to time left everyone apprehensive and the tensions were high. There were soldiers in every street corner and they guarded every main building with machine guns. Homeless children were sleeping in the streets in cardboard boxes. Pastors leaving their churches after Sunday evening service would disappear to never be seen again. Yet people were hungry for the Word and refused to allow fear to keep them away from the service. Thousands filled the stadium for the sunrise service, and a great number of them who had traveled from a distance slept out in the open air; come service time the place was electrified with praise.

On Easter Morning in one of the churches, Vasilis reluctantly assumed the pulpit for the message with a sense of apprehension due to his limitations with the language. He had prepared a brief message, which by the stretch of the imagination would not last longer than ten minutes. There was not enough knowledge of the language to leave his notes or to endeavor to illustrate. But as he began to share, something unusual took place. There was a freedom and an anointing that came upon him that to his astonishment and that of others, he preached for 45 minutes without lacking the proper words. God always surprises us when we are obedient. He always provides what is needed, the time that it is needed for His glory and the blessing of His people.

There was such warmth and such a moving of the Spirit of God at the closing of the service that one of the local pastors was observed having placed both his hands against the wall and rocking his head toward it, he was weeping uncontrollably. When Sister Nachtigall approached him and asked him what was the problem, his response was, "It is the word. It is the word. It has cut deep into my heart like a knife. I need to know what to do." Vasilis was sure and convinced of the destination that God had called him concerning the place of his missionary services, but he had no idea that there were a few detours in the process.

Alan Stewards says in an article, *God's Plan: Pure Gold*, "While the Lord may reveal our destination, He is under no obligation to explain His detours along the way." It could be that the Puritan preacher, Thomas Watson, had the detours of providence in mind when he said, "God is to be trusted when His providence seems to run contrary to His promises."[1]

There are times that God reshapes us, refines us and refits us for our final destination through the detours of His providence. That was the case with Vasilis and his trip to El Salvador.

The Salvadorian visit continued with an evening service in a remote village and a baptismal service in a lake which demonstrated the faith and the commitment of young Christians. These events melted Vasilis' heart and enabled him to sense the need for the liberating Gospel of Jesus Christ, "which is the power of God unto salvation to everyone who believes." He was not fully aware that God had planned longer and deeper detours before he reached his destination.

Kay and Vasilis were about to finish language school in San Jose, Costa Rica, and they were eager to set their sail for Argentina. It was not just their desire to engage in the work of their calling, but also they were tired of living out of the suitcases as they had for almost a year. It was during that time they received a call from the Missionary Board that their papers for Argentina were not ready and no one knew how long it would take. "Would they consider a year's assignment to Puerto Rico?" was the request from the Board. There were a Christian School and the Turabo Gardens Church there that were going through trying and testing times and there was a need for someone to bring stability and give direction.

Then Vasilis was invited to attend the Inter-American Conference of the Church of God in Latin America, which was about to convene in Caguas, Puerto Rico. At the same time, he could get acquainted with the situation of the church there. He does not remember many details about his visit with the church, except the people involved in leadership were not strangers to him. One was the son of his former professor at

Gulf Coast Bible College; the other was his classmate in the same place. He was delighted to meet representatives of the church and missionaries from the Spanish-speaking world. When a number of them raised the question to him, "How could a Greek speak Spanish without an accent?" his response was, "Well, when you speak the heavenly language, Greek, it is not difficult to speak the language of Amor – love, Spanish!"

There were several from the United States present for that conference including Vasilis' friend, Dr. Maurice Berquist, representing the Christian Brotherhood Hour. When Maurice was asked to address the assembly, he refused an interpreter. He said, "I just want to be like brother Vasilis, I want to speak in Spanish!" It was both inspiring and amusing to see the great preacher Maurice, struggling to find words to express his thoughts, especially for one who never lacked for the proper words, but Maurice would not be intimidated no matter what.

After the service, Vasilis put his arms around Maurice and said, "Maurice, all my life I wanted to see a great preacher to struggle and stutter through his message in the pulpit and today you made my day!" But he brushed it off with the response, "Vasilis, life is nothing but a dream." But this was Maurice Berquist and this is what made him so unique. He was not afraid of anything and he believed that through God's help he could do anything. It was these qualities in him that inspired Vasilis to never see obstacles in life but only opportunities.

The events and the experiences in Puerto Rico served as a confirmation that it appeared to be within God's will to minister there for one year, at least it appeared so since their papers for Argentina were not ready.

1. Alan Steward, *God's Plan: Pure Gold*, Pulpit Helps, October 2009, Vol. 34, No. 10, AMG.

THE SEASONING AND THE
SURPRISE OF A DETOUR

After language school, the family packed their eight suitcases and readied for their adventure in Puerto Rico. The flight schedule included two stops. One was in Panama City, where they got acquainted with the Panama Canal, and met pastor Taylor Mendoza and the church there. The second stop was Caracas, Venezuela, where they had to make connections. But the Caracas stop proved problematic. The travel agents failed to make reservations for the connecting flight. Therefore, there were not any seats available. Additionally, their suitcases were overweight. What made things even more complicated, they were running out of money. They did not have enough to stay in a motel or to pay for the overweight. So they huddled together there in the airport and prayed for a solution, then patiently waited for the outcome.

It was five minutes before the departure of the flight for Puerto Rico that their names were called to approach the desk. As Vasilis quickly ran there, the man said to him, "I do not know what happened, but there are four seats open, you will make your flight." Vasilis thanked him and then said, "What about our overweight?" His response was, "I do not have time to fool with it now, go on!" God is never late. He always keeps His promises and continues to amaze His people. His angel not only encamps around about those who fear Him, but also precedes them in their journey of faith.

The family finally arrived at the San Juan airport in Puerto Rico where they were welcomed by Earl and Freda Carver. They enjoyed their warm hospitality for a few days till they found a place to rent. It did not take long for them to realize the enormity of the challenge before them. Their faith, commitment, wisdom, relational tact and any administrative skills they might have, all were going to be put to the test. Vasilis recalls something humorous and he always shares it with a laugh, "My first missionary duty was performed when I helped Freda Carver take her Dalmatian dog to the vet. It was an emergency and no one else was around!" You see in the mission field you are not bound by your job description, you do what needs to be done as long as you do not forget why you are there.

Soon they became aware that they had to serve as pastors of the Turabo Garden Church that had gone through turmoil; as the administrators of the school whose future was uncertain and in financial trouble, serve as brokers in relationships and provide leadership in whatever areas they were called.

The Turabo Gardens Church in Caguas, Puerto Rico

One misty night about 10:00, realizing the magnitude of the challenge and his limitations, Vasilis took a stroll in the front yard of the church. As he was pacing back and forth, a question was racing through his mind, "What in the world am I doing here?" While the mist was cooling his face and pressing down on his hair, his heart was stopped by the response of the inner voice, "Just be here. Just be here!" Vasilis recalls that an overwhelming feeling of peace filled his soul and a confidence emerged which gave him the assurance that he was in the will of God and that God never fails. He accepted the purpose for which God had sent them there and it seemed as if God had provided a blueprint that night what to do next.

Some lady had told Vasilis the island of Puerto Rico was 100 miles long, 30 miles wide and it was resting on the top of a volcano cone in the middle of the ocean. Sarcastically Vasilis responded, "I want to make sure that I am standing on the right place. I do not want it to tip over. I cannot swim. Besides I came to solve problems and not cause them!"

Vasilis and Kay in the front of the Turabo Gardens Church 1977

God never commissions us without an adequate provision. He always sends His angels beforehand and touches the hearts of those who would serve as His providential angels on the stage of His activity to perform the acts of His grace and provision. There is no call, no matter how divine and certain, that is free from the attacks of the enemy or free from obstacles. When we keep our eyes on the goal and on Him who has set the goal, there is always victory according to God's definition. It is not our purpose to give a chronological list of all the events that took place in this detour, but simply to give a bird's eyeview of that which contributed to Vasilis' seasoning and of the surprises of God.

It was shortly after the family had arrived in Puerto Rico there was a line of tests that presented a challenge for them. The first test, three of their suitcases were lost and it took three months to locate them. Vasilis says, "There is one thing that we have learned; we have more than what we need and we can live as comfortable with less!" The second test, both Vaslis and Kay came down with "dengue", a sickness caused by a mosquito bite. It is a tiny creature in the mosquito family that when it bites, you do not feel anything, but the effects could be devastating. It takes every ounce of energy out of you and puts you in bed for a couple weeks. You do not want and you do not have the strength to do anything. Vasilis was flat on his back for two weeks, but Kay somehow managed to stay on her feet and keep up with the responsibilities such as taking the kids to school and looking after the church and the school.

The third challenge for them was the car they had just bought. It was a 1976 or 1977 Chevrolet Nova, which proved to be worse than a lemon. The whole year they were in Puerto Rico, they had weekly trouble and the mechanic had told Vasilis he needed to trash it. They could not exchange the car. Then Vasilis remembered reading an article in Reader's Digest concerning the introduction of that car in the Latin culture. Before it arrived on the market they promoted it as one of the most elegant cars and the name, Nova, sounded very impressive. When the car rolled into the Latin American market, nobody would touch it. They failed to understand the cultural implication of the name, Nova. The word "Nova" represents two words in Spanish. The word "no" which is the same as in English and the word "va" which is the conjugation of the verb "going" in the third person singular. What it communicated was this, "This car is not going." Would you buy a car that was not going anywhere? If Vasilis had remembered that article before he bought the car, it would have saved him from a lot of headaches.

A fourth test in the midst of so many things that were going on, Vasilis received a letter from Greece. The letter took about 15 days to get to him and explained that his mother was very ill and probably she was not going to survive. They had tried to get in touch with him through Spain and through the United States by phone to no avail. At that time Puerto Rico had a very poor telephone system. He tried to make contact but to no avail. He tried to make arrangement to go, but there were so many bases to cover and so many obstacles that after eight days he thought he could not make the trip, but he wanted to try one more time to make phone contact with his sister in Athens. After beginning at 10:00 p.m., finally at 2:00 a.m. the next morning he made contact where his sister's mother-in-law answered the phone. The bad news was that his mother had already died and his sister was on her way back home from the funeral. The only thing Vasilis could remember the rest of the night was her last words, "I will not see you again in this world."

Vasilis realized when he had said "Yes" to the Lord that it included his possible absence from significant events in the life of the family. It did not eliminate the pain but helps one to keep things in perspective. The fact remains, no matter what the circumstances or the happenings of life, or the place of our abode, we are never alone and never outside of His care. "Yea, though I walk through the valley of the shadow of death I will not fear, for Thou art with me, thy rod and thy staff they comfort me" (Psalm 23).

The fifth test that confronted them was the revelation that the school was going bankrupt! It had violated labor department laws and it was required to satisfy the labor department and pay 40 former employees retroactive wages for the past five years. Parents were in an uproar. Teachers were in chaos, and it appeared for certain that the demise of the school was coming. The Bible says in Proverbs, "When God is pleased with a man, He even makes his enemies to be friendly toward him!" The only thing that Vasilis could think was the promise that he had claimed for so long from the Old Testament where God says, "And my people shall never be ashamed!" Therefore he began to claim the promises of God and see opportunities in obstacles. He moved quickly to follow some steps that were impressed upon his mind. In the meantime, God had placed His providential angels in place and He had set the wheels in motion. When Vasilis thinks about the things that followed and the bold request that he had made, which appeared foolish to some people, he thinks he should have been laughed out of town.

He refused to raise tuition and asked the parents to raise it in a meeting. They gave him more than what was needed. He asked the teachers to stay with him to see the crisis through and promised them when things got better they will be the first ones to be rewarded. They agreed. He asked the Board to approve to add another grade, employed the service of an architect for a new floor over the cafeteria, asked the town newspaper to make a page available for promotion and without a dime to his name, they all agreed.

He went to the labor department and met with its head, Mrs. Catarjena, whose heart God had already touched, and asked her to send someone to investigate the school, with the promise, that if they found any improprieties, the would not fine them. She agreed. When she informed him the school had to pay the retroactive wages to all employees, he drafted forty letters offering the employees 20 percent of what was coming to them and asking them to donate the rest to the school or else the school would close and get nothing. She agreed. He sent the letter out, all the employees agreed with the exception of the former administrator and his wife. He went personally to the former administrator and made him a generous offer and asked him to agree like the others and drop his demands. He did not agree. Then Vasilis went back to the labor department and asked Mrs. Caterjerna to deny the former administrator and his wife any claims. When she asked Vasilis, "On what basis?" Vasilis without thinking, blurted out a phrase which he never thought or heard before. "On the basis of administrative deficiency," he said. "What is that?" asked Mrs. Caterjerna, to which Vasilis replied, "It was during his administration that the minimum wage was not paid and now he wants to be rewarded for it?" Her response elated Vasilis, "That is good for me!" There was victory on all fronts.

The only reason this story is shared here is to demonstrate that no matter how dire and difficult the situation there is a way out and negative things can turn to positive if we follow the directives of God and trust Him for the things that we do not know. Within ten months the school was in the clear, all bills paid, all materials and books bought for the following year, $10,500 in the bank, the plans for the building ready and a work group from the United States on its way to build!

God not only accomplished the purpose for which He had allowed them to take this detour, but also taught them some valuable lessons and He did it through the most unlikely people. He used an ex-drug addict Louis, to teach Vasilis how to do street evangelism. Vasilis recalls with a smile on his face the first time that Louis took him to a street corner and said to him, "This is where you will be preaching tonight!" So he stood there on the corner and began to preach to an imaginary crowd, hearing the echo of his voice and noticing the stares from those who were passing by.

By May of 1978 it appeared the Lord had brought to fruition the purpose for which He had allowed them to take this detour to the island of Puerto Rico. And it appeared that both the school and the church had regained both stability and direction. It was during that time that he received a letter from the Missionary Board with the request that since things were going so well in Puerto Rico for Vasilis and his family to remain there. Vasilis responded promptly and emphatically,

"No. God has called us to Argentina and to Argentina we shall go. We will be leaving Puerto Rico the end of May in order to finish our paper work for Argentina and get there by August." He sent them a plan of some of the things that needed to be done and a request for his replacement if possible to visit Puerto Rico before they left.

So before the middle of June they had said farewell to the wonderful people of Puerto Rico with a lively celebration, Puerto Rican style, and they arrived in the United States for the North American Convention and the preparation of the papers for Argentina. Since their papers were ready by the middle of July, Vasilis took about ten days to go to Greece and see his dad and mourn the death of his mother. Upon his return to the United States, the family set their sail for beautiful Argentina, the land of the gauchos.

SPIRITUAL ADVENTURE IN
THE LAND OF GAUCHOS – ARGENTINA

An Argentinian youth

Vasilis 1979

"Keep watch over yourselves and all the flock of which the Holy Spirit has made you overseers.   Be shepherds of the Church of God, which he bought with his own blood"

Acts 20:28 (NIV).

In August 1978 Vasilis and his family, armed with a sense of anticipation and apprehension, set their sail for South America. They felt God had called them for ministry in the country of Argentina. All of them felt somewhat comfortable with the use of the language and were excited about the possibilities there. It proved that both the details provided by the Missionary Board and their preparation for the task were inadequate. They did not even take into account that in arriving in Argentina in the middle of August, that it was winter there. They found out the hard way. While they tried to walk the streets of Buenos Aires with short sleeves, the local people were dressed with overcoats, hats and gloves.

Their immediate assignment was to arrive in Buenos Aires, get a motel, find a place to live and then, under the direction of the National Church, plant a church and provide leadership and direction for the National Church. They were given the telephone number of a church leader and the telephone number and address of a church organization leader, outside the Church of God, in Buenos Aires. They were assured these leaders could provide answers to their questions and some information about the conditions of the country. They were informed before they left the United States that both hotels and housing were cheap there, and they would not have any trouble. It came as a surprise to them that the inflation was 400-percent, the country was under military rule, and turmoil held reign. It is not that any of these things make any difference to God, but adequate information and preparation helps.

Their arrival in Buenos Aires greeted them with some surprises. As they went to the hotel, they found the cost was five times more than what they expected. When they had their first breakfast in Argentina, which consisted of four crescent rolls and four hot chocolates, it cost them $32.00.

Kay had an apprehension in putting the kids in the regular Spanish-speaking schools. After checking a couple of

English schools in the city she discovered the cost was beyond their means. The next morning as they had their devotions, Kay read Psalm 46, and in verses 10-11, read these words, "Be still and know that I am God, I will be exalted among the nations, I will be exalted in the earth! The Lord of host is with us; the God of Jacob is our refuge." The Lord used that scripture to remove the apprehension and the decision was made that the kids would attend the Argentinean public schools. They did not know at that time the Lord would not allow them to stay in Buenos Aires.

The search for housing proved to be more difficult and even disappointing. The anticipation was that they could find an apartment, which would cost between $250 and $300 a month, but the cheapest that they could find was between $1,100 and $1,200. All the circumstantial happenings and the voices were pointing that God might be closing the door for Buenos Aires. The next day one of the leaders of the Church from Alem, Misiones, came to Buenos Aires and visited with Vasilis and his family. He informed them that it would be difficult to stay in Buenos Aires. He was needed where the largest concentration of the church was and where the Bible Institute was located.

Vasilis, knowing in the missionary endeavor not only availability is important but also flexibility, accepted the wisdom coming from the church leadership and properly informed the Missionary Board, and they sailed in the direction that appeared God was leading. After waiting eight-and-a-half hours in the Aeroparque, the domestic airport in Buenos Aires, they boarded the airplane for Posadas, about an hour and twenty minutes' ride to Alem where they were supposed to stay. They settled for the night in an apartment in the basement of the Hogar de Los Ancianos, a home for the elderly. The next morning which was Sunday, they were scheduled to preach at the Obera Church of God, German Church, less than an hour from Alem. The morning began the celebrity status, everyone wanted to see and hear this Greek-American who had come as a missionary to Argentina. Sunday was memorable with great spirit and response, but Vasilis could not get away from the idea – here you had a Greek speaking in a German Church in Argentina, and he was speaking in Spanish.

On Sunday evening there was scheduled a combined

The church in Alem, Argentina

service between the German and the Spanish Churches in Alem. They were in the same compound, but with different buildings and the use of different languages. There was standing room only. Vasilis shared an enthusiastic and simple evangelistic message, which was warmly received by old and young alike. Identification with the young people was established that evening which proved very helpful later. Vasilis' evangelist approach with the students of the Bible Institute, in the surrounding area and throughout the country proved very effective. In fact it exceeded any expectation and resulted in some mass conversion of young people, which like a revival mobilized them.

One of the landmark events, which altered the attitude, outlook and outcome of the church, was the conversion of about 15 young people on Saturday evening during the national convention where Vasilis served as a speaker.

The congregation in Alem, Argentina, during the national conference.

Several of the young people entered the Bible Institute and the ministry. The second event was the initiative to ordain a number of young men, which proved to be a mixture of bitter and sweet. For some the act of ordination captured the heart, for others the head. The genuine ones moved forward and soared in ministry; the others, to use the words of the apostle Paul, "made a shipwreck" both of their live and ministry.

It appeared the Lord placed Vasilis and his family there in the role of catalysts, evangelists and teachers, which had an impact, both in Argentina, Uruguay and some in Chile. Due to his European background, his handling of the language and his identification with the common people and the culture, he was well accepted among the native Argentineans. He took a catalyst's approach when it came to church unity. There was a line of shrubs separating the Spanish church building from the German church building. One day Vasilis called a farmer to bring his tractor and together with some other brethren pulled up all the shrubs with the words, "We are not a Spanish Church or a German Church, we are one church, the Church of God." They used the one building to conduct children's church, which was under Kay's leadership with the help of some of the students from the Bible Institute, and the other for the regular

206

services with dual pastors, Vasilis' handling services in Spanish and Rudi Kunkle services in German. Both Vasilis and Kay taught in the Bible Institute, and Kay directed a choir in German without knowing how to speak a word of German! They led a group of 95 youth every Saturday and they traveled throughout the church in evangelistic meetings in all the providence, including Uruguay and Chile. .

**Kay conversing with fellow professors at
the Bible Institute**

ARGENTINA

The Argentinean experience was full of amazing things that the Spirit of the Lord worked in many different lives and situations which would take another book to describe. In the midst of all the exciting things taking place and in the midst of the serious, you would always find the humorous. For Vasilis and Kay, prayer was the main source of refuge in difficult times. But even in prayer, there are times that the humorous finds its way.

On a certain day they were traveling to an assignment a couple or three hours from Alem, and at noontime their car broke down as they were driving up on an elevated road. In spite of all their efforts, it would not start and there was no help in sight. They waited for a while and then tried again but to no avail. It was hot and in the middle of nowhere. So finally Kay said, "Let's pray, the Lord would help us to fix the car." Then she got behind the steering wheel and said to Vasilis, "Push." As Vasilis began to push up the hill, to their amazement the car started, and Kay took off in the car. From fear that it could stall again up the hill, she drove past the top on the other side. You guessed it right. Vasilis had to walk to catch up with her! They were able to find someone in the small town who repaired the car.

On another occasion during the rainy season, the car got stuck in the mud. In that part of the country the dirt is red. When it rains, due to the sliding of the mud, it is difficult to drive. Sometimes it is like driving on ice; other times the mud is so heavy the car would not move. They had a four-cylinder Renault. As they got stuck in the mud and the car would not move, Kay said, "I am going to get out and push," and she did. But standing directly behind the back wheel as it began to spin, Kay was covered with red mud. In a humorous spirit she extended both arms and said, "Look at me!"

There were times that circumstances demanded a direct intervention from God, otherwise the need could not have been met. In 1979 Vasilis was scheduled to speak at the Inter-American Conference of the Church of God in Latin America, which was meeting in Curitiba, Brazil. Fidel Zamorano was the originally-scheduled speaker, but due to some problems he could not make it, and they asked Vasilis to drive up from Argentina and speak. The night before their departure from Argentina, their son David was playing outside in the yard with some other boys. Suddenly David's stomach began to swell like a balloon and he had excruciating pain. They rushed him to a small Seventh Day Adventist Hospital outside of the town. After examination, their diagnosis was that his intestines had intertwined and that he should have emergency surgery. While the doctor left the room to go to make preparations for the surgery, Vasilis and Kay just looked at each other and said, "We have to be in Brazil tomorrow night. Let's pray that the Lord will take care of this." They knelt by David's bed and prayed. Then they sat and waited. Within thirty minutes there was a noise in David's stomach, the swelling went down and he was fine! They were able to make the trip without any problems.

While in Argentina, they lived under military rule. There were checkpoints everywhere. They had to produce the right documentation and cars were searched, causing some inconvenience. Vasilis never thought of bribing the guards but he was always polite and humorous with them. He and a friend from the church had driven to Posadas, about an hour-and-a-half from Alem to buy supplies. Among the things they had bought were some nice, juicy plums from Cordoba. They were tasty and very good. On the way back as they were approaching the checkpoint, he said to his friend, "Give me three plums and watch and see that the guard will not search our car!" As Vasilis stopped at the guard, he took a bite of one of the plums and upon looking at the guard, he said, "Oh, these are really good. Would you like to have a couple?" The guard responded, "Yes," took the plums with a "gracias" coming out of his lips, and he waved them off. Vasilis says, "This is not a bribe. It is generosity and compassion toward the guard, and he chose to return the favor. You did not promise anything, and you did not ask for anything! You make the call."

During the rule of the military in Argentina, a lot of ugly things took place and a lot of people suffered, and Vasilis was about to have a taste of what it was like. It had come out in Reader's Digest that 10,000 people had disappeared in Argentina, and no one knew their whereabouts. (After the military was out of power, the real truth came out what happened to those people). It was a few months before they would return to the United States that Vasilis had some business to take care of in Buenos Aires. He and the secretary-treasurer of the church, Soni, traveled to Buenos Aires. The second day there, they had finished their business early and decided before going to the hotel, to catch the train and go visit one of the pastors in one of the suburbs of Buenos Aires. They planned to then return to their hotel and depart the next morning.

It happened that the pastor was not at home, therefore, they had to turn around, catch the train and go back to their hotel. They did exactly that, but on the second train stop, as the doors opened automatically, the soldiers walked in with pointed guns and asked for documentation. Then they started pointing at individuals saying, "You, you, you and you, out!" Among those whom they took out were Vasilis and Soni. They made them sit on benches that were at the station and a soldier would guard each bench with the gun pointed at the people. Even though there was some fear and uncertainty, Vasilis loved adventure and he always liked to engage people no matter what the circumstances. He looked at the soldier that was guarding them, who appeared to be 18 or 19 years old and asked him, "How long have you been in the army?" The soldier responded, "Six months." "That is funny," said Vasilis, "I spent two years in the Greek army, and I never did a thing like this, pointing a gun at innocent people." By that time the soldier probably was shaking in his boots, but the shaking of his hands was visible.

They were loaded into the army trucks and they were taken to a police station where they stood up or sat down on the dirt in a fenced yard with guards. For the first time Vasilis found himself in a place with no rights whatsoever and without the ability to communicate with anyone. Vasilis engaged the policemen in conversation to no avail, except they were fascinated by the fact that a Greek was speaking Spanish. Past midnight, Vasilis looked at his friend, Soni and said to him, "You know, I read an article the other day that ten thousand Argentineans have disappeared and no one knows what happened to them." Then he looked Soni straight in the eyes and said, "I wonder if next week somebody would read that ten thousand and two have disappeared?" The funny thing of this whole ordeal was to pay for a hotel and then spend the night in a police station without a place to sit or lay down. That is a real adventure in life! They were released about nine o'clock the next day. The police had checked their papers and found that they were in the clear. "The only regret about the incident," says Vasilis, "is the fact that they failed to sing at midnight like Paul and Silas!"

The journey of faith is always mixed with the serious, the humorous, and the thundering manifestations of God's power. At other times there is His seemingly complete absence and silence. But through it all, there is the certainty of His companionship and His faithfulness in keeping His promises. On the humorous side, at one time Vasilis was traveling with brother Floral Lopez to an evangelistic campaign in Chaco. Floral was driving his car. It was about a nine-hour trip. They had not gone more than three or four hours into the trip when they had car trouble. They located a garage and after a wait of eight-and-a-half hours, the mechanic made the announcement that the car was ready and as he turned around to put his tools away, he picked up a piece of metal, he lifted it up so everybody could see it and asked, "And this?" He had forgotten to connect the fuel line! They made it for the meeting but a day late.

Mission Church in Chaco, Argentina

All the humorous and all the dangerous things with all their obstacles and difficulties are over-ridden by the glorious and positive things that took place by the grace of God. Vasilis and Kay recall that on a New Year's Eve about 90 young people got together for a life-imparting service. Dozens of

Transportation to the church in Chaco, Argentina 1979

them had been saved recently and shared their testimonies, sang choruses, washed feet and then with reverence and joy, gathered around the Lord's Table to celebrate Resurrection Power and take communion. What a glorious picture of the fellowship of the church! A great number of them found their way into ministry and the leadership of the church. There is no equal to the transforming power of the Gospel of Christ, and no greater contentment, satisfaction and rest can be found than living in the will of God and being led by His Spirit.

URUGUAY

Even though the involvement of Vasilis and Kay in Argentina required everything that they could master, they were not content without reaching to the surrounding countries for encouragement to the church and for evangelistic endeavors. Uruguay probably is the most secular country in South America and the Church of God has about three congregations there with the one located at San Grigorio, a small town that for the most part is surrounded by a river. This was a good place to take the students of the Bible Institute for an evangelistic expedition and practice. So it was there where they conducted revival meetings, Vacation Bible Schools, evangelistic outreach on the river beach, distribution of Christian literature and baptismal services. The trips were long and treacherous on gravel roads. The frequent flat tires appear humorous to us now but for them were both trying and dangerous. Night driving was very dangerous due to the multitude of all sorts of animals roaming around. One night while Vasilis was returning to Argentina, tall grass obscured any peripheral vision; a dog jumped in the front of the car and knocked out both headlights. The dog disappeared into the grass dead or alive, but Vasilis had to make it home without any lights. This was a scary thing indeed.

Travel to Uruguay, David and Jonathan

The baptismal services at the beach captured the curiosity of some of the people and demonstrated some seriousness and response. The distribution of literature was

214

received with reluctance and sarcasm. However, the impact of their effort was among the children and the youth.

The hostel accommodations for the group were grass huts that even for the Argentinean youth was a new experience. The hygiene environment probably should be left out of the discussion. You had to examine everything whether it was food or drink.

Baptismal in San Gregorio, Uruguay

Vasilis got the bright idea to order some chocolate milk and after he had taken a couple sips, he discovered there were two flies in it. When he protested, they brought him the second glass and assured him that there were no flies in it. When he had drunk half of the glass, there were flies in it, and even when they brought him the third glass, after finishing it, he found four flies in the bottom! You would think a fellow would learn and give up the idea of chocolate milk, wouldn't you?

VBS in San Grigorio, Uruguay

There is one thing for certain though, in spite of the tests, the obstacles, the humorous experiences, discomforts and the mixed reactions of people, the Gospel is still the power of God unto salvation to everyone who believes. Lives were transformed, the church was edified and the faithful Lavanderas have had a lasting ministry there.

THE CHILE EXPEDITION

Vasilis had received word there were some people in Santiago, Chile, and in some other towns who were reading the Messenger, a paper coming out of Corpus Christi, Texas. They were interested in the Church of God. He decided to make an investigating trip, which proved to be more frustrating than fruitful. Nevertheless, he made some contacts, gathered some information and became familiar with some personalities and perceptions. He met a single young man who had a radio program outside of Santiago, and who mainly was distributing literature provided by Evelyn Anderson from Corpus Christi, Texas. The second fellow was a family man in Santiago, who had a good job and claimed he had a house church and planned for Vasilis to meet with them that evening. He arrived there at the designated time, waited till 11:00 p.m., but no one showed up. Vasilis thought that there were some possibilities, but he had to return to Argentina.

As he arrived at the Santiago airport for his flight back to Argentina, he was not prepared for the reception that he received from the Argentinean Airlines. They refused to allow him to take a flight back to Argentina. His passport did not allow reentering the country. He had exited with his Argentinean Documents, which were not recognized for reentering purposes. Neither his explaining nor his begging was sufficient to change their minds. So he decided to take a break from pressing the issue and whisper a prayer. Then he approached another agent with new vigor and politeness saying, "Look, my family is in Argentina, my work is in Argentina, my resident papers are from Argentina, and one of your agents allowed me to get out of the country with the promise that I would not have any trouble returning. I did what I was told and now you tell me that I cannot return?" Finally with a smile, they allowed him to board the plane.

Even though his trip did not appear to be fruitful and his experience was not very pleasant, he felt impressed that he should return to Chile with some concrete plans and that someone from Argentina should accompany him. In the meantime, he kept in contact with the people he had met and there was some correspondence exchanged. He received an invitation from a gentleman, Zervantes, who was an ex-military and who had a small church meeting in a humble location. He and Soni traveled to Chile and the experience was a memorable one. It was wintertime in Santiago, which is located almost in the shadow of the snow-capped Andes Mountains. They decided to stay with the people. They were a very poor people, but very warm and with hospitable hearts.

Vasilis preached to a small lively group on Sunday morning with good response and enjoyed great fellowship in the humble quarters of the people. The evening proved to be a challenge for him. The room where he was lodging was built out of lumber boards and the wind could travel freely through the cracks. He was extremely cold, his teeth were chattering, his feet practically frozen and the only thing he had for cover was just a sheet. His host felt so sorry for him and she located an old small rubber thermos bottle with some warm water in an effort to warm his feet. Upon recalling some of the experiences, Vasilis always says with a smile, "Be careful what you say 'Yes" to. You might get it later."

The rest of the visit was spent with the other two contacts and gathering information. All three of them were invited and were assisted to attend the National Convention in Argentina, where they were introduced to the Church of God in Argentina. Their visit resulted in fraternal ties with the church in Argentina and they continued to maintain contact. When Vasilis and his family were returning from Argentina, they made a three-day visit to Santiago to renew contacts and provide encouragement. Vasilis was greatly surprised in 2008 when he was invited to speak in the Inter-American Conference of the Church of God in Latin America, which was hosted by the Church of God in Santiago, Chile, to find a church of four congregations, well-developed and on the move, but none of his original contacts were there.

Vasilis with the leaders of the Inter-American Conference in Santiago, Chile 2008

The journey of faith for Vasilis and his family in the land of the Gauchos was both eventful, rewarding, filled with divine interruptions and manifestations and an impact which determined the direction of the church in certain areas. Their exodus was not a permanent one. Upon the invitation of the church they have returned at least three times to minister to a wonderful and loving people. When God sets in motion the winds of His Spirit, change is inevitable both in personal lives and in institutions. One of the thing that amazes Vasilis the most and quite often makes him smile with gratitude, is that God would take a poor Greek boy from a remote village in Greece, transform him with His grace, anoint Him with His

Spirit, and then send him via U.S.A. to the land of the gauchos with the liberating message of the Gospel of Jesus Christ.

Children's Church in Argentina

You speak of adventure? You speak of reward? You speak of contentment, gratitude and praise? You speak of joy? It cannot get any better than that no matter how unimportant and insignificant one feels. Doing business with the King and for the King is the most satisfying engagement of the soul!

Baptismal in Argentina

Vasilis with Jonathan and David Iguazu Water Falls   **Kay at Iguazu Water Falls**

Vasilis with pastors in Argentina and representatives from Germany, Brazil, Chile, Uruguay and Paraguay

INTERMISSION AND REASIGNMENT

Vasilis receiving his Masters' from ETSU

"Let us go again and visit our brethren in every city, where we have preached the word of the Lord, and see how they do"

Acts 15:36 (NCRB).

Upon returning to the United States the family participated in the North American Convention and the World Conference in Anderson, Indiana. The Missionary Board had informed them that after their furlough to the United States, they wanted them not to return to Argentina, but to Montevideo, the capital of Uruguay with an expanded ministry to Argentina, Chile and beyond. They contemplated the offer of the Missionary Board, which had some merit, but in spite of the opportunity that it presented, they were not convinced it was God's will for their life. It was just a short time before that the family was due for a surprise. Kay was expecting their third son Daniel, who was born on November 11, 1980.

Since they had rendered their resignation from the Missionary Board effective December 30, 1980, they began to explore the options before them and in search of God's will. The had selected as a transitional place, Hamilton, Ohio, where Kay's sister Lillian and her husband Frank Ramey were pastor; so the family would be near them while Vasilis continued to travel on behalf of missions, and he did so for a year. Frank and Lillian proved to be God's providential angels for that period in many ways. Although several churches got in touch with them expressing an interest for them to become their pastors, Vasilis and Kay were very cautious. They did not want the need to make a living to be the driving force in their decision, but rather the certainty of God's will.

After a year of traveling, Vasilis and the family felt impressed of the Lord to accept the pastorate of the Tacoma Church of God in Johnson City, Tennessee. This was another station that the Lord had planned in their journey of faith. If we are obedient to the voice of God and live in the certainty of God's will there is no failure in life, in spite of the circumstances and there is no shame even if we suffer loss. For the greatest contribution and the greatest success in life is to do the will of the Father.

The pastorate in Johnson City not only provided them with a platform to minister to the congregation, but also a platform for ministry in the community, the state and a national and international scope. It was in this place that the whole family pursued their education, and Vasilis hosted a twelve-year radio ministry. Together they experienced some astonishing things of God's marvelous grace and the expression of His faithfulness.

In 1983 Vasilis, with some men from his congregation and Pastor Billy Franks with some men from his congregation in Shreveport, Louisiana and a representative from the Inter-American Conference of the Church of God, teamed together for a missions endeavor in Santo Domingo, Dominican Republic. The mission was to establish a Church of God and build a facility there. It was a wonderful week to see several come to know the Lord as Vasilis and others preached. The excitement was electrifying the last evening, as they met in the chapel that they just had finished for a worship service.

As 80 to 100 people lifted their voices to God in songs of praise and as one beheld the joy in their faces, the words of the apostle Paul were ringing like bells in their ears, "I am not ashamed of the Gospel of Christ, for it is the power of God unto salvation to everyone who believes, to the Jew first and also to the Greeks." Here there were humble people from different walks of life, from different cultures who went to the Dominican Republic to work with their hands and share with their heart the testimony of God's redeeming love with people that they had never met before. Here are the dynamics of the Gospel of Christ, it is shared, it is exemplified in love and in life, and then transforms the lives of those who believe. Vasilis and Kay made other speaking and working trips to the Dominican Republic with people from the Tacoma Church, and today there are more than ten congregations and a thriving school under the capable leadership of Gerardo Taron, a missionary from Argentina.

Missions never got off of the spiritual radar of Vasilis. It is not only that he continued his connection with other countries and often traveled there for speaking engagements and work camps, but also crisscrossed the country challenging congregations to respond to the Great Commission, and raising funds for missions, specially through Faith Promise Missions Conventions. You could hear him always say, "Missions is the lifeline of the church." In the congregations that he and Kay pastored, missions was the primary focus both in the local, national and international level. He always delighted in the risk of faith and there were times his faith appeared to be reckless, that if God had not come through it would have been a total embarrassment.

The story is related that when he arrived in Johnson City, the church was heavily in debt, and it had gone through some difficult times. He decided if they were going to have an effective ministry they had to get out from under the bondage of debt. He called his leadership and people together in prayer and shared with them. "We are going to pay our indebtedness off by the ninth of September." It was the first of March when he made that announcement and their debt was $120,000. Then he explained the approach. They were going to mail a letter out to everyone stating the vision, the need, the rationale why they needed to pay the debt off, and then trust God and wait on Him. Further, weekly they were going to report to the congregation on the progress and response in the church weekly newsletter. The Board agreed, although some of them reluctantly, but all supported the effort wholeheartedly.

The Crusaders S. S. Class at Tacoma

225

The letter went out on March 15th, not only to the congregation but all the people that were on the mailing list, from California to Alaska, to people who had some connection with the church. The church got excited, people began calling and asking questions and even strangers responded positively and in a generous way. But there were those who thought that such a vision was impossible in such a short time.

There was a couple who was quite new to the church. He was teaching at the East Tennessee State University. He was a high-ranking retired military man. He was also involved with Amway. He approached Vasilis and told him the only way he could realize his vision was to get the church involved with Amway. He

Vasilis at the parsonage

insisted on meeting with the Board of the Church. Vasilis would not have anything to do with it, but was very tactful. He informed the Board of his stand and then asked them to give him a hearing. After the Board had rejected his request and Vasilis communicated their response that it was not the right thing for the church to do, his response was, "The church will never pay its debt", and he left the church.

The Lord honors faith and sometimes reckless faith! On September 9th the debt was paid with $1,000 to spare. People responded from everywhere. When Vasilis announced the victory, immediately after the service his associate came to him and asked him, "Are you going to write a letter to Dr. Nelson and tell him what the church has accomplished so that he could know that he was wrong?" The response of Vasilis

226

was, "No, he reads the church newsletter, and he knows what has taken place, which is sufficient."

Vasilis had no idea of the role his ministry would play and the reason for which God placed him and his family in Johnson City. He always said that wherever God places you, no matter what the circumstances, just be faithful, He never makes mistakes and never rush God to accomplish what you think that should be accomplished. Make sure that you are in the center of His will and that you honor His word. All the rest will work out in His time.

He always claimed that in every station of his journey of faith, God had placed His providential angels in human form in order to assist him in the journey of faith and toward the fulfillment of His will. That was true also in Johnson City. Mike Clowers, a radio announcer in a local radio station and his parents, Glen and Sandra Clowers, helped to facilitate his radio ministry in that secular radio station, broadcasting his first and only religious program. Two years later, it was bought by a Christian and became a Christian station.

There were other providential angels who played a significant role in the purpose of God, whose particular contributions could not be expanded here, such as Glen and Helen, Ray, Frances, Hazel, George, Jeanetta, Bill, Mildred, Harry and Elsie. One of the phenomenal things that took place was the food distribution for those less fortunate under the direction of Sandra Williams, and with the help of the senior citizens team that

Vasilis with Daniel and Jonathan at the steps of the capital, Washington, DC 1982

227

provided food for almost four hundred families a month.

Both Vasilis and Kay were enjoying an effective ministry both within the church and the community as well as in other levels, and there was a certain feeling of contentment with quite a few plans unfolding for the future. There was no awareness in them that there was going to be a spiritual rumbling within them and that the Lord was going to redirect their sail. Kay had begun a career in nursing. Vasilis had finished a Master in Education Administration degree, and the two oldest boys had begun their college education.

David, Daniel and Jonathan at David's graduation from Anderson University

In the midst of such contentment and atmosphere for 14-and-a-half years, suddenly he and Kay felt release from the local ministry and accepted a sudden call that had come from another congregation. Both of them were convinced it was God's will in spite of the sacrifices that had entered the picture. The sacrifice appeared to be more acute for the youngest son, Daniel, who was about to begin his freshman year in high school, this was the only place that he knew. The decisions were made quickly, trusting God and not getting bothered too much with the details. But it soon became evident that they were embarking in one of the biggest challenges of their life and ministry.

Kay and Daniel left earlier due to the school situation. Vasilis remained behind to take care of the details and prepare the church for the transition. The last moments in this station of the journey were emotional. He wrote an open letter to the community, church and all, expressing his gratitude for their acceptance and support, and he got ready to assume the new sail for the journey of faith. The church had expressed all their graciousness and love in the farewell dinner before Daniel and Kay had left. Everything now was going to be stored in the book of memories and then venture out to create new ones.

His final act before he got in the car to drive away was to walk into the sanctuary of the church as darkness was falling outside. He slowly walked in the center aisle toward the platform, which was overshadowed by a cross in the background. Looking at the cross, he thanked God for all that had gone before and after him all those years. He thanked God for His mercy and power and he acknowledged that both His faithfulness and presence had accompanied them up to this point of the journey. As he knelt at the altar, only in the presence of the Lord and that of his own soul, words could never capture the emotions that were raging within. There at the altar he laid success and mistakes, people and plans and a congregation to which he had ministered for almost 15 years. He thanked God for all, committed all to His care, and that He who had guided them thus far in the journey was going to be with them the rest of the way.

As his lips pronounced a fated amen, his weak knees reluctantly made the effort to stand up, his heart was pounding with anticipation. He turned around to walk away toward new horizons with rejoicing and no regrets and the echo of His voice behind his ears, "And lo, I am with you always, even to the end of the ages."

THE BLUEGRASS ADVENTURE – WINCHESTER

Vasilis in Blue Country

"Love is patient, love is kind. It does not envy, it does not boast, it is not proud. It is not rude, it is not self-seeking, it is not easily angered, it keeps no record of wrongs. Love does not delight in evil but rejoices with the Truth. It always protects, always trusts, always hopes, always perseveres. Love never fails"

I Corinthians 13:4-8 (NIV).

The family had enjoyed a fruitful ministry in Johnson City for almost 15 years. It had become like home. The two boys had finished high school in this place. The youngest one was following in their footsteps in sports and was about to enter high school as a freshman. They had just bought their first home four years before and Kay was settled in her career as a nurse. There was not any thought for any move. He had ignored several invitations for other pastorates. In fact they felt that a sense of permanency was settling in their life.

It was in the early summer of 1995 that their world changed drastically. There was no awareness that the Lord had another station for Vasilis' journey. He had just returned from Greece, where he preached his dad's funeral. There was a sober reflection over him; he pondered the fact that he had spent so little time with his parents and now they were both gone. Going home would not be the same again, even though he had two brothers and a sister with whom there is a bond of unconditional love. Their support and prayer for his ministry had always been manifested in different ways, but the absence of parents always leaves a void.

Even though Vasilis was greatly blessed in the ministry with many opportunities and the favor of His presence and His Spirit, he always was consumed with a challenge that there was something more in ministry. He wanted to be driven by passion in ministry and not just performing professional duties. There were times that both Vasilis and Kay thought that they might return to the mission field. But there was not a serious thought given for a decision. For now they were content with the challenge of the ministry, their involvement with the church at large and their occasional trips to various mission fields in the form of work camps or preaching and teaching endeavors. It was evident that the missionary burden had claimed their hearts forever.

It was during that time and under such circumstances that the call came from the First Church of God in Winchester,

Kentucky, a well-known congregation in the Church of God for its leadership and strength. Even though they had resisted such calls before, something prompted them to say, "Yes." A first and a second visit to the congregation confirmed the will of God and the call was extended to them. There was no second thought, neither in the beginning nor at the end about whether or not the move was the will of God.

There is something though that we quite often overlook. We live with the misconception that when we respond to the call of God and His will that all will go well; that there will not be any obstacles, any difficulties or problems. It is true that wherever God guides, He provides. It is also true that if we are faithful and obedient to the call of God and His will, He will enable us to fulfill the purpose for which He has called us. What is not true though is that our faith would not be tested, our soul would not be tried and that we would not experience the roars of the enemy of our soul. What is not true is that we would not experience persistent warfare, when at times it appears the enemy is having the upper hand. There is something greatly missing in the church of the West with the promotional concept of a Gospel of health, wealth and that we would be free from suffering!

This is neither the teaching of Jesus nor that of the New Testament. Jesus said, "In the world you will have tribulations, but be cheerful, I have overcome the world" (John 16:33 NKJV). Paul says, "Those who live godly shall suffer persecution" (2 Tim. 3:12 *paraphrase mine).* It is to that end the Bible states it takes patience to do the will of God. The Christian or the minister who shies or tries to avoid sacrifice and suffering, will have difficulty to empathize with those who suffer and fully experience total dependence upon the Lord and sense the nearness of His presence. The church is purified, united and grows during persecution and suffering.

They were not fully aware that the level of ministry to which God had called them, that they were embarking on a new challenge and that their faith, commitment and faithfulness were going to be tested in different levels. For the moment, they were overtaken by the vision the Lord had set before them and by the possibilities that were about to unfold. There was not time to think of obstacles, difficulties or the unexpected. After all the motto has been, "If God be for us, who can be against us." They had faced challenges before and even crises, and the Lord always came through and sometimes even in miraculous ways. God had overthrown strongholds of the enemy before and in whatever station God had called them in the journey of faith, He always had placed His providential angels for assistance.

The move to Winchester was made in September of 1995. Although the exit from Johnson City was easy and went smoothly, their entrance to Winchester met with some logistical obstacles. These obstacles contributed to their effort to be more trusting on the Lord. It was difficult for them to locate housing. In fact their first year in Winchester, they had to move three times before they built their house. The following month after the move, Kay lost her mother and there were other events which kept the family on the edge, but there was no doubt of the call. In fact, all the happenings were confirming the call and the awareness that Satan was on the attack, wanting to interrupt God's plan.

In the midst of all these challenging events that surrounded them and others which were about to follow, Vasilis was led to spend time with the book of Nehemiah, which the Lord used Nehemiah mightily to both inspire him and outline the steps of progress that he should take in order to walk within the blueprint that God had for the church. This book not only inspired a series of messages to challenge the congregation, but also it enabled Vasilis to reshape, recast and redefine the vision for the building and the relocation of the church.

Even though he had some directives and preferences on what should be done, he decided to proceed with the plan set in motion by the congregation and wait on the Lord to intervene if that was His intended purpose. When the plan reached a dead end, then he presented the alternative plan that appeared to be from the Lord as to the direction that they should follow. It was accepted and followed to its completion. From the moment that the architectural plans were changed, both the leadership and the congregation embraced the challenge and for almost two years it appeared that the hand of the Lord was directing the whole project into its victorious conclusion. He stated once, "I have never been involved in anything like it. Even though I was a participant and a major player in the process, I felt like a bystander and that someone else was in charge and directing the process. It was the most satisfying and peaceful feeling to know that someone else, higher than human leadership, was in charge."

There was no doubt for them that one of the purposes for which God sent them to Winchester was the building and the smooth relocation of the church. It is almost ironic that in the journey of faith on the world stage, God would lead him to this stage for such a unique experience. The church had envisioned building for a long time. They had bought 43 acres of land, had spent $110,000 in architect's fees for a multipurpose building, but for some mysterious reason progress stalled and faith was faltering. Vasilis had agreed with the plans of the congregation and he had expressed his willingness to go forward with the project. But he was like Nehemiah, he had not told anyone what was in his heart, and that is, that he did not feel that the present plans was the best thing for the congregation. Instead of talking to the leadership about it, he decided to talk to the Lord. He wanted the Lord to make the changes and not he.

In the meantime he was waiting for the right time and for the manner in which the Lord was going to lead into the new direction. There were no bids offered the first time the plans were put out for bid. There were only three bids second time the plans were put out, and all of them were much higher than the church had anticipated.

This surprise caused the leadership to start looking for alternatives and changes. A meeting with the architect did not prove very helpful in solving the dilemma. It was at that time Vasilis felt God was leading to make the move, a rather dangerous faith move. He recommended that the architect be released from his duties as well as all those who were involved in the building process. Then he asked the leadership to ask the congregation to suggest 30 names out of which the Church Council was going to select 12 by unanimous vote, which would constitute the new building committee and come up with a new building plan which could be both suitable and affordable to the needs of the congregation. The new committee was given three months to come up with a concept. The congregation was both pleased and very supportive of the new approach.

While work was taking place toward the new concept, Vasilis recommended the congregation build a pavilion on the new property and begin some activities. That was going to inspire confidence in the people that the leadership was serious both for building and relocation. The project was wholeheartedly accepted and things were set in motion. Changing course and reshaping the vision in the middle of the process is not easy and at times, it can be very dangerous, but when God is leading it is the best and only thing that you can do. The new concept was presented to the church in due time, it received a 98 percent approval and the 45,900 square foot building was completed in March of 1999.

On March 28, Palm Sunday, the church organized a car procession from the old church to the new, where each one received a palm branch before they entered the building. A young girl who was staying with her grandmother in the town of Winchester, looking out of the window and seeing the big procession of cars, turned to her grandmother and asked,

"Grandma, who died? Surely, whosoever died, he must have had a lot of friends." The grandmother was both prompt and quick to make the correction, "Honey, nobody died. It is the First Church of God moving into their new building on Colby Road." You never have to fight for changes when God goes before you and prepares the way. The Bible says, "Unless the Lord build a house, in vain work the laborers." The building and the people were dedicated to the Lord on the first Sunday of May 1999.

The First Church of God in Winchester was and still is serving as the host church for Pastors' Fellowship. Upon assuming the pastorate, Vasilis became the chair of the Steering Committee of Pastors' Fellowship. Pastors' Fellowship came into existence a little over 37 years ago and consists of ministers and lay people who ascribe to the message of holiness and who endeavor to remain true to those biblical truths which gave birth to the Reformation Movement of the Church of God.

The formation of Pastors' Fellowship was caused by the perception of some and the reality in others that the Church of God Movement was abandoning the biblical truth which gave it birth. Therefore, they were organized with the sole purpose of re-teaching, re-preaching and re-stating those biblical truths and calling the church into account.

Vasilis, upon assuming the chair of Pastors' Fellowship, sought to raise its scope to the national level with the positive emphasis of being true to the biblical truth and exemplifying the spirit of holiness and participation and cooperation.

Vasilis comments that, "truth and holiness unites people and that the Holy Spirit or His gifts never war with each other but rather complement each other for the building of the kingdom and the edification of the church." He surrendered the chairmanship of Pastors' Fellowship in 2008 with the prayer and hope that the biblical truths which gave birth to the

Reformation Movement of the Church of God would lead us to the practice of unity, holiness and Biblical authority.

The Winchester stage of ministry thrust Vasilis into the larger church in various forms: member of the Board of Trustees of Mid-America Christian University, Vice Chair of the National General Assembly of the Church of God, Vice Chair of the Kentucky General Assembly, and a greater involvement with the missions outreach of the church with evangelistic endeavors and work camps in Mexico. There were preaching and teaching engagements in Argentina and the Inter-American Conference. Then there were joint adventures with Pastors' Fellowship to Argentina upon the request of the church for teaching, preaching and printed materials where he was accompanied by Richard Bradley, Allan Hutchinson and Don Neace and his son, DJ, with rewarding results.

In this station of the journey of faith Vasilis experienced tests, trials and obstacles as well as the triumph of sustaining Grace. As stated before there is a misconception in the life of a lot of professing Christians and sometimes in the life of some of God's ministers, that if you are in the will of God, if you are obedient to His word and faithful to His calling, that all will go well. There would not be any difficulties, no oppositions and no obstacles and that peace and prosperity would prevail on every hand! But even though God promises to be with us, to protect us and provide for us, the above concept could not be further from the truth.

The spiritual warfare, the opposition and the obstacles come stronger to those who have definite marching orders from the Lord and who are not willing to bend to the left or the right. Only those can know the true trying of the soul and can see the hand of God providing the triumphant deliverance like the angel of the Lord did for Peter while in prison. It was in this particular stage on this station of the journey of faith that the enemy launched its attack and the spiritual warfare began. Vasilis' youngest son, Daniel, a star athlete, suddenly became seriously ill with a diagnosis that did not look very promising. Kay's dad, who had come to live with them, was dying and Kay took a medical leave of absence to care for both her son and her Dad. There were other things too numerous to mention here which, like dark clouds, seemed to cover the rays of hope. There were times that Vasilis would drive at midnight from the hospital, while Kay stayed with Daniel. Upon arrival at the house, he lay flat on his stomach on the floor of his office praying for direction.

The whole series of events appeared to the little souls that there was unfolding the punishment of God to someone who has been unfaithful. Vasilis knew the enemy had unleashed all its fiery darts thinking he could prevail without taking into account that "the angel of the Lord encamps around about those who fear Him." No matter how dark, the light is always brighter in the darkness, and God gives us a song in the night. God's people always are led into victory no matter what happens. God demonstrated His faithfulness to Vasilis who had claimed His Word to Abraham years before when he left his homeland to follow the call of God, "I will bless those who bless you and curse those that curse you and I will make you a blessing." Vasilis testifies that all the challenges of the spiritual warfare became steppingstones to triumph, which fortified character and faithfulness.

As it has been in every station of the journey of faith, God had placed His providential angels in this station who provided the necessary assistance, some aware and others totally unaware, but all led by the hand of divine providence that directs the path of His children with the promise, "My presence shall go with you" and "I have sent my angel before you."

Those unnamed angels whom God used to minister to Vasilis and his family in this station of the journey may not mean anything to the reader or to others, but they were known both by God and to them: Eugene, Finley, Woodie, Peggy,

Carol, Carolyn, Charlie, Betty, Jean, Imogene, Carolyn, Bob, Ed, Ralph, Paul, Wayne and a host of others whose names are in the book of remembrance.

In this station of the journey of faith, both Vasilis and Kay felt the leading of God, the contentment of being in the will of God, and the faithful rewards of the Grace of God. Both of them were convinced that Winchester would be their last pastoral experience. Their multiple positive experiences there can make a book by themselves.

In 2006 Vasilis and Kay felt the Lord would have them terminate their pastorate in Winchester by the end of 2007. Without having any definite plans about anything, they began getting ready for the next station of the journey of faith the Lord had prepared for them. It was a mutual agreement that Vasilis should engage in ministry with the church at large as the Lord provided the opportunity and then do some writing. They quickly sold their house within three weeks, rented a small house close to the church. They began seeking the direction of the Lord and waiting for His marching orders. When everything became clear, in September of 2007, they announced their intent to retire from the pastoral ministry by the end of November of the same year. They were going to relocate in Johnson City, Tennessee, and from there they would pursue whatever doors God would open.

Upon making the announcement to the church about their intent and the potential future ministry, their younger son Daniel asked Vasilis, "How are you going to get invitations for meetings? Are you going to advertise? How would people know?" Vasilis responded to him as follows. "For over forty years of ministry, God has led and provided and opened doors beyond our imagination or expectation. Not once have we ever asked to go or to preach anywhere. The Lord knows our name. He knows our address, and He knows how He wants to use our life. He knows both our needs and the gifts that He has given and He will open the doors He wants us to walk through. We

239

will wait on Him and we will trust Him." God honored such a faith and indeed He has been faithful in fulfilling His promises.

The conclusion of their ministry with the First Church of God in Winchester was a smooth transition. The church expressed their graciousness and love in many tangible ways, special services with special guests for the occasion, dinner and reception and the display of a lot of things which brought to mind God's faithfulness and the love of a people who love God and His Kingdom and who sought to be faithful to His word and do His will. It was an emotional but releasing experience, sensing the smile of God's approval and envisioning the manner in which He was going to express His faithfulness in the future. In the meantime, the words began to resound once more, "Hitherto has the Lord helped us" and "If God be for us, who can be against us."

THE JOURNEY OF FAITH CONTINUES

Vasilis and Kay

"But without faith it is impossible to please Him, for He who comes to God must believe that He is, and that He is a rewarder of those who diligently seek Him"

(Hebrews 11:6 NKJV). "Looking unto Jesus, the author and finisher of our faith, who for the joy that was set before Him endured the cross, despising the shame, and has sat down at the right hand of the throne of God" (Hebrews 12:2 NKJV).

Faith is interwoven in everything in life, but there are times that an extra measure of it is manifested or exercised for doing that which is outside the realm of the norm. It was that extra faith that caused Abraham to leave his home not knowing where he as going and to take the difficult steps to proceed toward the sacrifice of his son. It was that extra faith that enabled Moses to refuse to be called the son of Pharaoh's daughter and suffer reproach with God's people rather than to have the pleasures of sin for a season.

The spectrum of life is full with that extra measure of faith that stands as a beacon light to guide and inspire, raise our hopes and to challenge us to take the risk, leap into the unknown and trust God. One only needs to read the eleventh chapter of Hebrews and suddenly his path will be illuminated with such beacon lights of faith. Enemies are overcome, obstacles are overthrown, difficulties are endured and weaknesses become strengths due to the employment of this extraordinary faith.

The last two years of Vasilis and Kay's pastorate, even though they were enjoying it tremendously and had a measure of security and useful involvement, quite often it was invaded with a measure of restlessness, a feeling that God was calling for a change and a new adventure. What gave some validation was the fact the feeling was mutual. It was the inner feeling that they should make themselves available and then let faith and God outline the adventure for the rest of the journey.

So, on the 25th of November 2007, the chapter of the journey of faith at the Winchester station was closed. A new chapter began with the faith that God leads His children along. It has been three years since that eventful decision and the Lord has been faithful in honoring His promises and in opening doors that would honor Him and provide the ministry that He intended for them. There have been many doors opened across the country and even beyond its borders. So the journey of faith continues. To what extent and for how long, that rests only with Him who said, "I will never leave you nor forsake you." As for Vasilis, he will continue to stand by the door, ready to respond to the call of God either to some field for service or to the new home in glory!

In May 2010 there were three of his books published, *The Holy Spirit Within Us*, *The God Who Is*, and *Leadership, Laity and Heresies*. Other works completed at the present are *Vasilis*, which you hold in your hands, *The Virtues of a Healthy Church*, *Rediscovering the Master and Discipleship*, *A Word in Due Season for People in the Church*, *Soul Searching Devotions*, *The Kingdom of God and the Millennium*, *Sobering Thoughts for Changing Times* and *Piercing the Darkness with Rays of Truth*.

As the journey of faith continues, who knows the encounters that it might bring and the surprises that it might hold? There is one thing for certain though, "His eyes are still on the sparrow, and I know He watches over me!"

A PARENTHESIS: THE HUMOROUS, THE ASTONISHING AND THE PROVIDENTIAL

Baptismal at Jordan River, Vasilis, Jim Chapman, and Frank Ramey

"The Lord is my rock, and my fortress, and my deliverer; The God of my rock; in him will I trust: He is my shield, and the horn of my salvation, my high tower, and my refuge, my saviour, thou savest me.

As for God, his way is perfect; the word of the Lord is tried: He is a buckler to all them that trust in him"

(II Samuel 22:2-3, 31 NCRB).

The journey of faith has been long and it is so full of adventure that is almost impossible to deal with details; even with the most significant events. But it might be a little helpful if some of the humorous, the astonishing and the providential is shared as the memory facilitates. There was a simplicity and sincerity in Vasilis' life as well as to his approach to life that sometimes may appear to defy common sense. During his early childhood, there was a certain amount of mischievousness, and there were times he was not as truthful as he should have been.

In the early years of his life and their humble dwelling when his mother would make a variety of cookies for some special occasion, the only way that she could safeguard them from different creatures that could find their way into the house and from the children, specially Vasilis, was to line a basket inside with clean towels, place the cookies in it, then cover it with clean towels and with a rope, hang it from one of the house rafters, out of the reach of all. When the family was gone, Vasilis always found a way to reach the cookies and savor their flavor. When his mother would discover with embarrassment the absence of the cookies when she tried to serve a visitor and asked what happened to the cookies, Vasilis eagerly and promptly blamed the rats or the mice, until he was caught! You do not want to know the rest of the story.

When Vasilis was about nine or so years old, he was rather strong willed, and he was trying to assert his personal independence, when his oldest brother asked him to complete a family chore. They were living out in the country and he asked Vasilis to take a bucket and go to the well and draw some water. Vasilis refused and the brother insisted. He took the budget and placed it in Vasilis' hand and then his on the top, holding both Vasilis' hand and the handle of the bucket and led him or rather dragged him to the well. He asked him to hook the bucket to the chain and lower it to the well for the water. He again refused. Then he took Vasilis' hand and forced him to hook the bucket, lower it down to the well and then raise it up full of water. Then he put it in Vasilis' hand and asked him to carry it home. He again refused. He again put the handle of the bucket in Vasilis' hand and on the top of it his own and forcefully they began the walk toward the house. About halfway to the house, the patience of the older brother had run out. He grabbed the bucket of water and poured it over Vasilis' head, and then put the bucket on his head like a hat! Who won or what do you call this: independence, strong will or pure stubbornness? You make the call.

On one occasion when Vasilis was about ten years old, they were living in a small rental house close to the school. Vasilis was determined to stand up for himself. He and his oldest brother were in the house and they were involved in some kind of discussion, which was more or less a heated disagreement. Vasilis does not recall

Vasilis with his brother Thanasis at the well 1976

what it was all about. He looked around the house and noticed that one of the windows was open and in the front of it was a bed. So he got the bright idea that he would push his brother down on the floor, jump on the bed, then on the window and then out of the house. He thought it was a workable plan. He pushed his brother, jumped on the bed and while the one foot was resting on the window and the other in the air, to his horror he felt someone grabbing the foot in the air and pulling him down off the bed! I do not think you want to know the rest of the story.

When you are in the mission field, in a different culture, different country and different language, you could experience a lot of funny and serious things, and sometimes very embarrassing things. While in Argentina Vasilis conducted his first wedding in Spanish and he did his best to do everything well, after all there was a Greek-American performing a marriage ceremony in Argentina. Everyone came to see and the church was packed. During the ceremony, he noticed his wife was trying to get his attention, but he was so preoccupied in doing things well that he did not pay attention. He failed to ask the people to sit down, so they stood the whole ceremony thinking that it was an American custom, and they did so with both grace and dignity. Oops! It can happen to the best of us.

It was on Sunday evening in Argentina after the service that Vasilis, Rudi Kunkle and Arturo Shultz were engaging in a conversation in the front of the building. As people were passing by and some of them standing or visiting with others. The day before there was ministers' meeting, and they all had agreed to do certain things, with the agreement that they would talk about the details on Sunday evening after the service. It was this matter that Vasilis was discussing with Rudi and Arturo, who informed Vasilis that the matter under consideration was cancelled. Vasilis responded with an elevated voice, "What? Who changed it? I would like to know, when all of us together decide on something, who has the power to change it? I want to meet that person." As Vasilis turned around he noticed a red-faced businessman was staring at him. They never told him who he was, but a picture is worth a thousand words. Sometimes it does not pay to verbalize your thoughts, especially when people are around. It is not good PR.

Kay was always vocalizing her faith about God's faithfulness and God's provision. While they were students at

Asbury Seminary, their journey was a journey of faith, and God had astonished both of them with His grace and faithfulness. There was a pastor friend who was graduating from Asbury College and was going to the mission field. They wanted to have him and his family for dinner before they left, but things were tight. Their cash was about $25.00, which was needed for travel to fill the speaking engagement for that weekend. Kay said, "I am going to use it for the dinner and the Lord will provide." She did the necessary purchase and on her way back to the school apartment, she was thinking about the needs for the weekend. Upon arriving at the apartment, the mailman passed by and handed her an envelope. Yes, you guessed it right, inside there was a check for $25.00! Did God provide? They think He did.

One of the funny things happened in Vasilis' family during the German-Italian War. Close to the end of the war where both Germans and Italians were defeated and they were running for their lives. It was summertime and most of the Greeks take a nap at noontime. Some days before, there was a furious battle raging in a town of about an hour-and-a-half from Vasilis' village. On that particular day while Vasilis' dad was taking a nap, the church bell began to ring and the message to the men of the village was to run for help, the Germans were coming. Vasilis' dad jumped out of bed grabbed his pants with one hand and his shepherd's stick with the other, and ran out of the door while his mother was standing by the door saying to his dad, "Dino, it is war. What do you think you are going to do with your pants in your hands and with a stick?" Several times in later years, it made the family roll with laughter.

On a particular preaching trip to Argentina with Richard Bradley, Allan Hutchinson, Don Neace and his son DJ, Vasilis served as a translator while they were preaching. Richard Bradley was preaching on the story of Adam and Eve and how God took a rib out of Adam's side and He made Eve. Now in Spanish there are two words that share a similarity and if one is

248

not careful there can be embarrassment. The word costilla –
rib, and the word parilla – grill. So as Richard was preaching
and said, "And God took a rib out of the side of Adam and
made Eve", Vasilis promptly translated it into the Spanish, "Y
Dios saco una parilla de lado de Adam Y hizo a Eva" – "And
God took a grill out of Adam's side and He made
Eve." It was only when the crowd began to roll with laughter
that he realized the error of the tongue. Can you feel for him?

**Vasilis witnessing to a
monk at Mt. Olympus,
Greece**

**Vasilis with his oldest niece
Tula and his brother
Christos**

**Vasilis and Kay
at Bethlehem**

Vasilis at Mt. Olivet   **Vasilis with Israeli soldiers at East Jerusalem**

Vasilis with his uncle Yianis and his dad Dinos

RETROSPECTIVE REFLECTIONS

Vasilis reflecting as he views the sea and the mountains

Vasilis sitting at the steps of his birthplace

"Nevertheless I am not ashamed, for I know on whom I have believed and I am persuaded that He is able to keep what I have committed to Him until that day"

II Timothy 1:12 (NKJV).

"I have fought the food fight, I have finished the race, I have kept the faith. Finally, there is laid up for me the crown of righteousness, which the Lord, the righteous judge, will give to me on that Day, and not to me only but also to all who have loved His appearing"

II Timothy 4:7-8 (NKJV).

As we come to the close of this adventurous journey of faith, which has been touched by the Big Story of God's redeeming love and grace, it is normal to sit at the setting of the sun and reflect on things that have been done. But reflections when true and honest, sometimes are filled with praise and thanksgiving; other times they are marked with sadness and tears, and still there are other times when they are decorated with confessions, regrets and even repentance. So, let's start with a true confession: Vasilis and the author are one and the same person, in case you had not figured it out by now. Vasilis is my Greek first name, and I have used it to tell the story in the third person due to my dislike of the use of I, me, my and mine. Even though it has been difficult to treat Vasilis as someone else, it has eliminated some of the emotional stress.

It would have been impossible to visit all the details of the story. The effort has been to follow the journey of faith by pointing to some of its steps and visiting some of its stations, and then giving an overview how God can use almost anything to guide a life, lead it to His will and use it for His glory.

The sun still sets and rises over the small village, Agridion, but almost everything else has changed with the exception of its serenity, pictorial panorama, hospitality and the towering mountains that surround. There is an occasional panigiri where expatriates, villagers and visitors gather for a couple days of celebration. The gushing waters of the vrisi have been diverted to provide running water for the houses that remain. The village is no longer dark; lights illuminate a few of its places. There are roads where cars can come in from two different directions. The noise at the vrisi has died out, no flock to water and no lively conversation or the noise of the children splashing in the water. The church bells still ring out, but not as loud or as often. There is no resident priest anymore, and the school building is empty, only renovated to be a reminder of the past. It still has a small cofenio where old and wrinkled faces gather for conversation and long to entertain a visitor, even a total stranger.

Sitting with your conscience at the setting of the sun and reflecting on the things you have done is the most sobering experience. It will not be true to say that there have not been sighs, smiles, tears, questions and a lot of thanks. There is astonished gratitude to God for His grace and His faithfulness as well as for those providential angels who filled their posts so well in helping a fellow pilgrim fulfill his pilgrimage. Oh, yes, there are some regrets, but none of them can take away the awe that the soul feels concerning the faithfulness of God, the overshadowing of His presence and the leadership of His hand and His Spirit.

Sitting at the setting of the sun and reflecting over six decades away from the village and all that has transpired you are bound to raise some hypothetical questions such as "What if?" Even though a great preacher has said that the word "if" is the most useless word in the human language, nevertheless a lot of us use it more often than we like to. "What if" Thanasis had not taken the initiative to relocate the family during the civil war? "What if" a New Testament was never given to Vasilis? "What if" Nick Zazanis had not visited Vasilis in the hospital? "What if" the young person from Iowa had never sent him the magazine REACH? "What if" Verna Joiner had never answered his letter? There are so many "ifs" that we can fill pages with them, but the fact remains that God honors faith, fulfills His promises and brings His will to pass. There is no doubt that it has been a most thrilling and adventurous journey. No one could ever imagine that God would give the honor and the privilege to a poor boy from a remote village to roam the world with the Good News, and be blessed and bless. What a privilege to have people of different cultures, languages and nations to call them brothers and sisters and feel the warmth of their embrace, bound with the love and the spirit of the King of kings and Lord of lords.

What can be greater than that? You think of gratitude, praise and thanksgiving. I have been blessed! If only I could be used by God to be a blessing to others, a fraction of what others have blessed my life, there will be no regrets.

As I sit overlooking this mountainous village at the setting of the sun, the question echoes through my soul and mind, Amazing grace how could it be that God would choose a boy like me! Amazing grace has been my comfort, courage and joy to always look at your face. There is nothing I can boast on, except on His Mercy, redeeming Love and Sustaining Grace.

As the rays of the setting sun slowly begin to sink behind the mountains in the West, the assuring word echoes in my mind, "We have come thus far by faith, leaning on the Lord", and there is another song that rings within me, "Someday the silver cord will break, And I no more as now shall sing. But, oh the joy when I shall awake within the palace of the King! And I shall see Him face- to- face, And tell the story- saved by [His] grace..."

The sun has disappeared behind the mountains while the heart beats faster and thoughts race through the mind. But no one knows what the next sunrise would bring or where it would find us, except the certainty that overrides all uncertainties, "His eye is on the sparrow, and I know He watches over me. I sing because I am happy, I sing because I am free; for His eye is on the sparrow, and I know He watches over me!"

"Blessing and glory and wisdom, Thanksgiving and honor and power and might, Be to our God forever and ever. Amen" Revelation 7:12 (NKJV).

PHOTO GALLERY OF VASILS' FAMILY

Vasilis' father with oldest granddaughter, Tula

Vasilis' uncle Yianis and his cousin Yeota

Vasilis and his father

**Vasilis' sister, Yeota, with her husband Sakis
and their children Mimi and Niki**

**Kay's parents Evalee &
Walter Matney**

**Kay's sister, Leda &
husband David**

Kay, Daniel, Jonathan, Vasilis and David at home

**Vasilis and Kay with his father, mother, brother and sister
in Greece 1967**

257

Vasilis and Kay with her two sisters Linda and Lillian with their husbands Kenny and Frank in Greece 2000

Vasilis with father and mother, two brothers and sister, Thanasis' wife, Eleni, with their four children, Tula, Dina, Stefanos and Elias, and Vasilis' cousin with his wife and son in 1959

Kay and Vasilis in
the front of the
church in
Amaliada, Greece

Daniel with his grandfather,
Dino in Greece 1993.

Vasilis and Kay with their son Jonathan and Vasilis'
brothers and sister at Mid-American Christian
University in 1999 upon receiving his honorary
doctorate

259

**Vasilis' father with Kay, Jonathan, David and
Daniel in Amaliada, Greece, 1989**

**Vasilis' grandchildren,
Sam and Anna.**

Soteroula and Thanasis

Bill Konstantopoulos immigrated to the United States as a student in 1962. He is a graduate of Gulf Coast Bible College, now Mid-America Christian University. He studied at Asbury Seminary, at Fuller Seminary he did In Service Training and graduated from the language school in San Jose, Costa Rica. He earned a Master in Education Administration from East Tennessee State University and in 1999 Mid-America Christian University awarded him an Honorary Doctorate.

Bill has served the church more than four decades as pastor, missionary, evangelist, educator and leader both in the state and national level. He and his wife Kay have three grown children, Jonathan, David, Daniel and two grandchildren, Sam and Anna and continue to minister in camp meetings, ministers' meetings, revivals, and missions conventions.